DE-CLOAKING
The HOLY GHOST

De-Cloaking The Holy Ghost

Copyright © 2015 Dr. Larry T. Barnett, Sr. All rights reserved.

No rights claimed for public domain material, all rights reserved. No parts of this publication may be reproduced, stored in any retrieval system, or transmitted in any form or by any means, electronic, mechanical, recording, or otherwise, without the prior written permission of the author. Violations may be subject to civil or criminal penalties.

Library of Congress Number: 2015958496

ISBN: 978-1-63308-201-4 (hardback)
        978-1-63308-199-4 (paperback)
        978-1-63308-200-7 (ebook)

Cover & Interior Design by R'tor John D. Maghuyop

1028 S Bishop Avenue, Dept. 178
Rolla, MO 65401

Printed in United States of America

Dr. Larry T. Barnett, Sr.

DE-CLOAKING
The HOLY
GHOST

BAPTISM IN THE
HOLY SPIRIT

CHALFANT ECKERT
PUBLISHING

TABLE OF CONTENTS

Foreword 7
Acknowledgments 9
Prologue 11
Introduction 17
Historical Perspective 21
What Is the Holy Ghost? 25
Interminable Baptism in the Holy Ghost 33
The Free Gift of the Holy Ghost 39
Conversion or Baptism in the Spirit 43
No More Tarrying 47
The Gifts of the Spirit 51
Why the Controversy? 59
It's Time to Set the Record Straight 63
Do They All Speak with Tongues? 69
The Gifts of the Spirit 77
The Gift of Tongues 85
The Gift of Interpretation 87
The Gift of Prophecy 89
The Gift of Wisdom 93
The Word of Knowledge 95
The Gift of Discerning Spirits 99
The Gift of Faith 103
The Gift of Healings 105
The Working of Miracles 107
Conclusion 109
Bibliography 113
Appendix 115
Scriptural References 149
Biblical Figures and Places 155
Index 159
About the Author 161

FOREWORD

The misunderstanding of and inaccurate teaching about the Holy Ghost has caused significant spiritual damage to many. Tragically, it is possible to pass down old traditions and mindsets that leave seekers not only bewildered but afraid. Given the way some church leaders and Christians are prone to describe the "Holy Ghost," it's a wonder anyone wants it at all.

What is it? Is it for us today? What does the Holy Ghost look or feel like? Why does it seem so hard to obtain? Will I ever get it? This book is a tool, not only a spiritual primer, but a way of understanding the Holy Spirit that answers many questions and dispels countless myths. While the Holy Ghost is perhaps the least-understood, at the same time it is one of the most mocked and disparaged core Christian tenets.

If you've ever been frustrated with what you know about the Holy Ghost, ever wondered if it is real or even secretly longed to have a spiritual encounter with God — this book is for you. This book is a down-to-earth, up-to-the-minute manual on the path to spiritual transformation. Aptly titled, *De-Cloaking the Holy Ghost*, Dr. Barnett does a superb job of demystifying the Holy Ghost by providing a practical and biblical hands-on resource for assisting all of us in gaining understanding and greater insight. My hope is that you don't simply read this book, but that it prompts you to say yes to

God. So, I want to invite you to go on a journey, let the book be your roadmap: Not that you can simply learn about God but that you will experience Him in ways that you never dreamed possible.

Dr. Ron Webb
Author, *Destroying the Root of Racism*
Author, *Leadership From Behind the Scenes*

ACKNOWLEDGMENTS

This labor of love could not have been done without the support and encouragement of many truly wonderful people that God placed in my life. I'm grateful for the late Pastor Calvin Watson and Mother Marva Watson Clemons for leading me to Christ and for having the courage to defy denominationalism, and for operating in the gifts of the Spirit.

Thank God for my five children: Cala, who went home to be with the Lord much too early for her mother and me, Shaya (her husband Michael), TJ (his wife Christina), Sean (his wife Christine), and Donte; and for my two grandchildren Daja and Michael Jr.

I'm extremely appreciative of all the saints at St. John Praise & Worship Center Ministries International for sharing the visions and journey that God has provided for thirty years.

I would certainly be remiss in failing to recognize my brother, Anthony (his wife, Janet), who was not only my big brother and protector but friend and an ardent supporter. Praise God for giving me a sister-in-law, Royce, who has been more of a sister than an in-law, and my nephews Anthony Jr. and Caleb, who are more like my sons. I'm also indebted to my mother-in-law, Mattie Grundy, who has treated me like a son and supported me over the years. Thanks are also due to Betty Jo Barnett, my stepmother, who has supported me

Acknowledgments

with many prayers. I owe much thanks to Yolanda Simon who unselfishly edited this manuscript just because she is my sister, friend, and co-laborer in the gospel of Jesus Christ.

There are three people that I need to acknowledge, without whom I could not be the person that God has allowed me to become. First my precious mother, the late Betty Mae Ridley Barnett, whose prayers, love, and commitment would not allow me to settle for mediocrity. I'm grateful for my Dad, Burdis Barnett, Jr., who was the hero that slept next door. My parent's undying devotion and great sacrifices paved the way for me to obtain an education they never had opportunities to pursue. Thanks, Mom and Dad, for protecting me from the mean streets of Chicago, myself, and the plans of the adversary and for raising me to be a man who loves God and his family.

Finally, the most important person that I need to honor and pay tribute to is my best friend and wife of more than thirty-five years, the beautiful, the lovely, the wonderful woman of God, and my best friend, Carol Jean Grundy Barnett. Thank you for giving me back to God and for allowing me the time to research and write this book. Thank you for your support, encouragement, and for truly being my best friend on the planet, next to Jesus.

Needless to say, I give all the praise, glory, and honor to my Lord and Savior, Jesus the Christ, without whom I would be nothing at all.

PROLOGUE

In the Spring, 1977, I experienced the single most important event in my life. Although growing up in a home where my brother and I were taught to believe in the existence of God, I had no true relationship with the risen Savior. To say that I was lost would certainly be an understatement. In love with the world and pursing all of its pleasures with vigor and tenacity, the last thing on my mind was being a true Christian. Somehow I believed that the mercies and graciousness of God would allow me a pass to get into His Kingdom. Even though I only went to church services on special occasions, if asked, I would have described myself as a Christian. Despite the fact that I only thought of Jesus when I was in trouble, desperate, or wanted something, I felt as though I was somehow okay. However, I was groping in spiritual darkness and separated from the love of God. At that point my priorities centered around the pursuit of personal gain, pleasures, and being who and what I thought I wanted to become. Unbeknownst to me, God had a different plan.

In 1977, I was a sophomore at Southern Illinois University in Carbondale, Illinois. The demands of college life and the rigors of study pretty much consumed most of my day and left little time for a social life, and no time for God. It was during this time that the Lord began to put people and situations in my life that caused me to not only acknowledge

His very presence, but to know that the course I was on could only lead to death, hell and destruction. It seemed as though everywhere I turned someone was talking about Jesus and end time prophecies being fulfilled. If I turned on the television, Billy Graham or Jack Van Impe would just happen to be on the telecast, imploring people to prepare for a savior who was soon to return. My own mother, who has since gone home to be with the Lord, would be singing a spiritual song or hymn. Her voice, so beautiful and strong, would fill the house with an anointing from God that would penetrate the darkness of my heart. Even my family members were somehow being used by God to get my attention.

One particular Sunday, my Aunt Dorothy persuaded me to go to a church service with her. We went to a small country church in rural Southern Illinois called Second Baptist. Although the sign said Baptist, it was not what I was expecting. People were praising the Lord boisterously! There was shouting, dancing, and people speaking in a language that was not of this earth. They obviously had something that I had never experienced. Even though I went reluctantly, I found myself focusing on the message and the movement of the Spirit of God upon the members of that congregation. After the message, I felt touched and convicted, but not ready to give my life to the Lord on that level. I was still willing to pray over my food, go to church services every now and then, and even sow seeds in the offering, but I was not willing to be a "holy roller!" My plan was to live rowdy and have a good time until I reached an advanced age and no longer enjoyed that kind of lifestyle. At the end of the service, an announcement was made that this church was hosting a weeklong revival beginning on the preceding Monday. For me, the invitation to attend went in one ear and out of the other. I had no intention of making a return visit.

On Monday afternoon when I returned home from SIU, my mother, once again, was singing one of her hymns. After relaxing a bit, I decided to watch whatever was on television. As soon as the set was on, I could hear a preacher powerfully delivering a message of salvation through the shed blood of Jesus. It was at this point that I felt the Spirit of God urging me to go back to that little country church in Tamms, Illinois. When I arrived, the service was already in progress. Although I cannot remember the songs that were being performed or the subject of the message, Jesus was speaking directly to me, inviting me to come in to Him and offering to come in to me. The love of Christ was so powerful, a peace and assurance swept over me that I had never experienced. Suddenly I found myself at the altar weeping, repenting, and asking Jesus to be my Savior. That was the greatest event in my life! I had been changed, washed, and born again into the Kingdom of God!

Not long after my salvation, I began to read and study the Word of God with diligence and hunger. The more I read, the more I wanted to read. Regardless as to the demands of the university, I would stay up late studying my Bible and trying to understand what God was saying to humanity. During my studies, I kept seeing a connecting string between salvation, power, authority, and anointing. At the center of this connecting string was the Holy Ghost. Over and over again I would read about the power the early church possessed and how the Apostles operated in the miraculous. I would ask the pastor and the members of that little country church in

Tamms to share the experience they had with being baptized in the Holy Spirit. Coincidently, I became a member of that church. While everyone was kind and tried to help me understand what they experienced, how they felt, and what the Holy Ghost meant to them, I seemed to be unable to fully grasp the whole movement. I began to pray, fast, and ask God to help me understand what I was seeing in his Word as well as in the lives of my new family. I wanted to be saved on Bible order and experience everything that was available to the Household of Faith.

It became my passion and my journey to be baptized in the Spirit. I was thoroughly convinced that this phenomenon was not only real, but relevant and available to today's Christians. I went to every revival and "tarrying" service that I was aware of, regardless of denominational affiliations. In some services they would anoint me with oil and lay hands on me, praying with zeal and passion that I be filled with the Holy Ghost. In one ear a passionate saint would instruct me to, "Hold on!" In the other ear another zealous saint would instruct me to, "Let go!" Needless to say, I was quite torn — which would I do, hold on or let go? In other meetings they would stand me up and ask, "Have you been living free from sin?" Immediately I would begin rehearsing the events of my behavior through my mind. I didn't curse, swear, smoke, or drink any alcoholic beverages today. I don't remember any unkind words, or disparaging remarks. As far as I could remember, at least for that day, I just couldn't recollect doing anything to upset Jesus. In other meetings I would attend, the preacher would lay hands with great authority commanding me to be filled with the Holy Ghost, although at times it felt more like a slap than laying on hands. They would then tap me gently under my chin and tell me to repeat the name of Jesus. While there were times when I felt like something was about to happen, I walked away from those services feeling empty and spiritually inept. It seemed as though my life was in conflict with the practices of Spirit-filled saints and the Word of God, which for me was quite a conundrum. Even though I knew I was indeed born again, I felt as though something was somehow spiritually wrong with me. Perhaps I had been too wicked prior to salvation and therefore disqualified from "full membership" in the body of Christ. Maybe I wasn't dedicated enough or simply had underdeveloped faith. Surely there had to be something wrong with me personally, especially when there were others who became saved after me who seemed to be filled with the Holy Ghost immediately after they were born again.

For whatever reason, I was lured into the trap that so many others have fallen into, that is the erroneous belief or teaching that suggests the baptism in the Holy Ghost is an exclusive privilege left to those who have somehow merited it. Many zealous adherents to the Holy Ghost experience have somehow created an illusion that only the "super saved and sanctified" can receive the phenomenon of being immersed in the Spirit of God, with the evidence of miraculous signs. Somehow we have failed to convey that the baptism in the Holy Ghost is a gift that has been reserved for those who have been transformed by the blood of the Lamb. The Holy Ghost cannot be earned, purchased, or controlled by the flesh of humanity.

For years the gift of the Spirit has been shrouded and cloaked in religion, disbelief, misunderstanding, and mystery.

Prologue

Since the birthing of the New Testament Church, many have sought to control, hide, and ignore the baptism in the Holy Ghost. My personal quest to be filled with the Spirit of God, like the 120 believers who were gathered together when the day of Pentecost was fully come and finally receiving this precious gift, has motivated me to "De-Cloak" the Holy Ghost, not by works, religion, or imagination but by sharing a gift that is open and free to the children of God.

It was only after I gave up my own preconceived notions as to how the baptism in the Holy Ghost would take place that I understood that He had been waiting for me all along. It was in the quiet of my then pastor's living room that I relinquished my will and expectations for His. Without fanfare, religious surroundings or ceremony, the Spirit of God completely overwhelmed me and began to minister to my spirit with the evidence of signs and wonders.

INTRODUCTION

Growing up in the '60s and '70s, the author of this work was an avid *Star Trek* fan. One of the biggest threats and adversaries to Captain Kirk and the crew of the Starship *Enterprise* were the Klingons and their warship, known as the *Bird of Prey*.

Although the Klingons were fierce warriors particularly known for their war lust, it was the *Bird of Prey* that was the most fascinating. It had the amazing ability to cloak itself in invisibility. While "cloaked," it was impossible for the *Enterprise* to pinpoint its location. This may have seemed like an excellent advantage, but it had one major drawback. While "cloaked," the *Bird of Prey* lost the ability to use its offensive weapons. As soon as it fired its weapons, it became visible and, therefore, vulnerable to an assault by the *Enterprise*.

Like the *Bird of Prey*, the Holy Ghost has been "cloaked" by religion and misinformation. Educated and uneducated Christians, church-folk, theologians, clergy, lay people, and satan have all done an outstanding job of "cloaking" the Holy Ghost in invisibility and obscurity. Misunderstanding, miseducation, and debate seem to create more controversy about this aspect of God's purpose and work than any other issue. While many followers of Christ apparently have no problem accepting the fact that the Holy Ghost is part of the oneness of God, there seems to be a lack of consistency regarding

Introduction

the activity and manifestation of His work in contemporary times. In some regards, He only exists as a figurehead whose work was completed on the day of Pentecost.

The Word of God clearly states, "For God is not the author of confusion but of peace, as in all churches of the saints." (1 Corinthians 14:33) Why then does there seem to be so much mystery, confusion, and feelings of uneasiness regarding the promise and operation of the Holy Ghost? From denomination to denomination, and often within denominations, there are different interpretations and understandings of the person, function, and presence of the Holy Ghost.

DE-CLOAKING THE HOLY GHOST

An In-Depth Study of the Baptism in the Holy Ghost

HISTORICAL PERSPECTIVE

If we truly want to walk in the fullness of the Spirit and live a victorious life for Christ, we must "de-cloak" the Holy Ghost and fire our offensive weapons. It is the purpose of this study to provide clarity regarding the baptism, purpose, and status of the Holy Ghost.

In Acts 1:8, Jesus made the following promise and declaration, "But ye shall receive power, after that the Holy Ghost is come upon you…" On the day of Pentecost, the promise and delivery of the Holy Ghost was fulfilled. All believers shared the same experience; they were all filled with the Holy Ghost and all spoke with other tongues as they were empowered by His presence. Throughout the book of Acts, there are other accounts of born again believers who received the same gift and experienced speaking in tongues (or glossolalia). While there was no apparent controversy at this point regarding the authenticity of the Paraclete, or gift of the Holy Ghost, there is evidence that not every believer had knowledge of His existence. "He said unto them, have ye received the Holy Ghost since ye believed? And they said unto him, we have not so much as heard whether there be any Holy Ghost." (Acts 19:2) The first century church regarded the Holy Ghost as part of the Triune God.

Gary Gilley (2010) in his book, *A Study In The Holy Spirit*, noted five major periods of historical developments

Historical Perspective

in the doctrine, ideologies, teachings, and practices regarding the Holy Ghost.

The first period, Montanism, occurred in the 2nd century. Montanus was a Christian convert who began his prophetic activity from AD 135 to as late as AD 177 (Robeck, 2010). Montanus believed that he was a prophet of God and that the Holy Ghost spoke through him. The adherents of Montanism, also known as the New Prophecy, believed in the person of the Holy Ghost and sought to infuse the church with new life. According to Gilley (2010), Montanism went beyond the scriptures and declared that the "age of the Paraclete" had come and with it new revelations from God. The Montanists believed in the spontaneity of the Spirit and that there were prophecies and revelations that existed outside the scriptures. They believed that their authority by virtue of the Paraclete exceeded that of the early apostles. They embraced a strict standard of ethics and were initially embraced by some members of the orthodox community, but were eventually labeled as heretics (Robeck, 2010).

The second historical development of the doctrine of the Holy Ghost came about during the 3rd century and was known as Monarchianism or Sabellianism. Sabellius was a theologian and priest who taught during that century. His basic tenets were the oneness of God, and that God did not exist as a trinity. Monarchism is also known as modalism and teaches that the progressive being of God was first manifested as Father, then son in the form of Jesus, and today is expressed as the Holy Ghost. They do not believe in the Godhead, which exists as three distinct coexistent eternal persons. "Sabellius championed a form of Monarchianism, called modalism, which taught that the Trinity was a manifestation of form rather than essence. In other words, God was in the mode of the Father in the Old Testament, Jesus in the New Testament, and the Holy Spirit today. According to modalism, there are not three persons within the Godhead, but One who manifested Himself in different forms. The Holy Spirit would be the role that God is playing out today. Modalism survives today in the Oneness Pentecostal circles." (Gilley, 2010)

Monarchianism was followed in the 4th century by Arianism. Arius taught that Jesus was a created being subordinate to God and not necessarily a deity. Like Monarchianism, Arianism rejected Trinitarian ideas and theology. The Council of Nicaea, AD 325, was forced to convene to deal with the issues created by Arius (Gilley, 2010). Arianism was rejected and condemned by the council, except for its views on the Holy Ghost, which taught that He was, indeed, deity.

Fifty-six years after the Council of Nicaea, the church yet again struggled with the issues of the deity of Jesus and the Holy Ghost. According to Gilley:

"The Council of Constantinople was convened in 381 to deal with these issues. While the Council took a strong position on Christ, it did not clearly elucidate the essence of the Holy Spirit or His relationship with the other members of the Trinity. The Synod of Toledo was called in 589 to settle the question of whether the Spirit proceeded from the Father only or from both the Father and the Son. The Synod determined that the Spirit proceeded from both and this was accepted by the Western Church. The Eastern Church, however, would

not accept the Synod's decision (believing the Spirit proceeded only from the Father). This issue resulted in a church split, known as the Great Schism, which has never been mended." (Gilley, 2010)

During the 17th century, a group known as the Socinians, named after Fausto Socinus, denied the pre-existence of the Son and believed that the Holy Ghost was simply an energy sent by God and not a person. Consequently, He had no deity or being. Influences of Socinianism can yet be seen in cults and groups in contemporary times.

Needless to say, a great chasm continues to exist regarding the Triune God and even more specifically, the Paraclete. The person and ministry of the Holy Ghost is yet under scrutiny and debate as of this writing.

WHAT IS THE HOLY GHOST?

It is the contention of this writer that the Holy Ghost is not a "what" or an "it." The Holy Ghost is a WHO! According to Easton's Bible Dictionary (p. 568, 1897), the Holy Ghost is defined as:

> "The third Person of the adorable Trinity. His personality is proved (1) from the fact that the attributes of personality, as intelligence and volition, are ascribed to him (John 14:17, 26; 15:26; 1 Corinthians 2:10, 11; 12:11). He reproves, helps, glorifies, and intercedes (John 16:7-13; Romans 8:26). (2) He executes the offices peculiar only to a person. The very nature of these offices involves personal distinction (Luke 12:12; Acts 5:32; 15:28; 16:6; 28:25; 1 Corinthians 2:13; Hebrews 2:4; 3:7; 2 Peter 1:21).

Whereas God in the person of Jesus, the Christ, was born to the Virgin Mary and manifested Himself in the flesh of humanity, God the Holy Ghost came or was sent to us in His divine nature to indwell those who have been born again. It was the distinct assignment of the Holy Ghost to bear witness of the work accomplished by the vicarious suffering and supreme sacrifice of Jesus.

What Is the Holy Ghost?

It is important that we remember that the Holy Ghost is, indeed, God Himself in the Spirit and, therefore, has the sovereignty to make assignments and demands on our lives. The decision making of the Holy Ghost is prevalent throughout scriptures. In the book of Acts, the Apostle Peter declared that it was the Holy Ghost who decided to lay no further burdens on new converts other than to abstain from eating food sacrificed to idols, and from blood, and from things strangled (Acts 15:28-29). They were also admonished to keep themselves from fornication by the edicts of the Holy Ghost. It was also the Holy Ghost who forbade the Apostle Paul from preaching in Asia.

The Holy Ghost is a revealer and a teacher. It was the Holy Ghost who revealed to the early saints the great things that God has in store for those who love Him. He also revealed or divulged the things of God in a manner that was comprehensible by mankind. We can only know the wisdom of God and have the ability to compare spiritual with spiritual through the teaching of the Holy Ghost.

Even the spiritual gifts that we divinely receive are based upon the will of the Holy Ghost. "God also bearing them witness, both with signs and wonders, and with divers miracles, and gifts of the Holy Ghost, according to His own will." (Hebrews 2:4) Even the prophetic word of God was not the work of man, but came as a result of the will of the Holy Ghost.

Easton's Bible Dictionary (1897) asserts that:

"His divinity is established (1) from the fact that the names of God are ascribed to Him (Exodus 17:7; Psalms 95:7; compare Hebrews 3:7-11)*; and (2) that divine attributes are also ascribed*

*to Him, omnipresence (*Psalms 139:7; Ephesians 2:17, 18; 1 Corinthians 12:13); *omniscience* (1 Corinthians 2:10, 11); *omnipotence* (Luke 1:35; Romans 8:11); *eternity* (Hebrews 2:4). *(3) Creation is ascribed to Him* (Genesis 1:2; Job 26:13; Psalms 104:30), *and the working of miracles* (Matthew 12:28; 1 Corinthians 12:9-11). *(4) Worship is required and ascribed to Him* (Isaiah 6:3; Acts 28:25; Romans 9:1; Revelation 1:4; Matthew 28:19)."

During the 40 years of wandering, murmuring, and rebelling, the children of Israel knew whether or not Jehovah God in the person of the Holy Spirit was with them or not. Although it may not seem to be clear in the book of Exodus, the New Testament book of Hebrews makes it quite obvious that the Holy Ghost they referred to as God was the deity in question.

Throughout the Old and New testaments, the Holy Ghost is intertwined and part of the completeness of God the Father and God the Son. Although different in work or function, there is no subordinance or separation, neither is there any indication in the scriptures that the Holy Ghost is anything less than divine deity.

While theologians and clerics may debate the issue of the "Holy Trinity," it is quite conclusive that the Holy Ghost is the Spirit of the living God. He is the third person in the Triune God. The Holy Ghost is referenced at least 90 times in the New Testament alone. Although the words Holy Spirit only appear in the Old Testament three times, there are numerous references to the Spirit of the living God. He can be found from Genesis through Revelation.

What Is the Holy Ghost?

In John Sherrill's book, *They Speak With Other Tongues* (1985), he provides the following definition and characteristic for the word spirit:

> *"The root word for 'spirit' in Hebrew is 'Ruah' and this word has two distinct meanings. One is 'wind.' And the other is 'breath.' One is an impersonal force, the other is much more intimate, assuming consciousness and awareness, for you cannot have breath without having someone who breathes. The basic quality of both, however, was movement. Ruah was always in action; it was moving. It affected everything with which it came in contact. Another concept inherent in the ancient use of the word was creativity. Ruah was intimately associated with breath. It was the Spirit of God that moved upon the face of the water at Creation. It was the breath of life breathed into the nostrils which made man a living soul." (p. 118)*

In the New Testament, the word Spirit is translated from the Greek word pneuma, from which we get the term *pneumatology* or theology of the Holy Ghost, which is the life-giving force or breath. *Strong's Concordance* Greek lexicon entry 4151, defines Pneuma as the third person of the Triune God, coequal, coeternal with the Father and the Son. He is the vital principal by which the body is animated; a gentle blast of wind or movement of air. As the "air" of creation, Job declared that we are made by the Spirit. "The Spirit of God hath made me, and the breath of the Almighty hath given me life." (Job 33:4)

We can safely conclude that the evidence is overwhelming in establishing the fact that the Holy Ghost is a real moving, breathing, creative person. The Holy Ruah or Pneuma is yet moving today as He did in Creation and in the making of man. Praise God, there is no mystery as to the existence of the Spirit.

The Holy Ghost is not a creation of the New Testament church. He, like Jesus, is God and, therefore, has always been. The Apostle John tells us, "For there are three that bear record in heaven, the Father, the Word [Jesus], and the Holy Spirit; and these three are one." (1 John 5:7) The terms Holy Ghost and Holy Spirit will be used interchangeably in this study. To argue which term is more appropriate is simply a lesson in semantics.

In addition to being a WHO, the Holy Ghost is also a gift. In the book of Acts, the Apostle Peter rebuked Simon the Sorcerer because he wanted to buy the Holy Ghost. In Peter's reprimand he states, "…Thy money perish with thee, because thou hast thought that the GIFT of God may be purchased with money." (Acts 8:20)

Jesus also promised the gift of the Spirit during His earthly ministry. In the gospel according to John 14:16 and 17, Jesus encouraged his disciples prior to his crucifixion with these words, "And I will pray the Father, and He shall give you another Comforter, that He may abide with you forever; even the Spirit of truth whom the world cannot receive, because it seeth Him not, neither knoweth Him: but ye know him; for He dwelleth with you, and shall be in you."

The fulfillment of the promise occurred when the day of Pentecost was fully come as recorded in the second chapter of Acts. Outside of being regenerated by the Spirit and being indwelt by Him, it is impossible to know or understand Him or His work because of the limitations of the flesh. As much as God is a Triune being, we have been created by Him in His image and likeness. We are comprised of body, soul, and spirit. "And the very God of peace sanctify you wholly; and I pray God your whole spirit and soul and body be preserved blameless unto the coming of our Lord Jesus Christ." (1 Thessalonians 5:23) We are, in essence, a trichotomy. The ontological trichotomy of man would indicate that while we exist in three interdependent parts, each has a sphere of influence and operation.

In the Old Testament book of Exodus, God describes the Tabernacle as having three primary parts: the outer court, the tabernacle, and the holiest of holies. Like the Tabernacle, we consist of the outer court, the body; the tabernacle, the soul; and the holiest of holies, the spirit. In the Greek, we are Soma (body), Psuche or Psyche (soul), and Pneuma (spirit). In his book, *Dispensational Truths*, Clarence Larkin (1920) used the following diagram to illustrate the trichotomy of man:

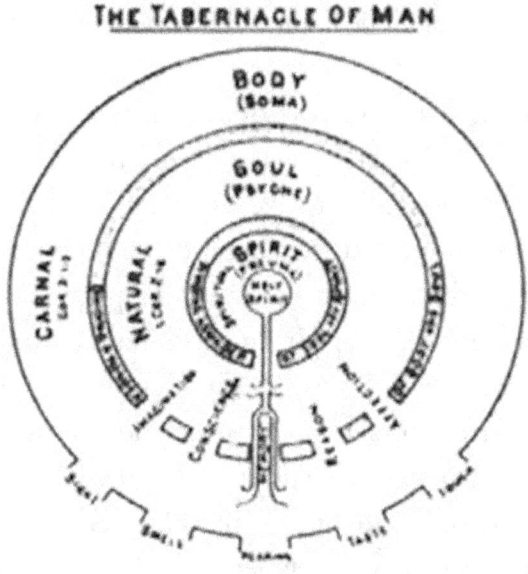

The physical nature of man is bound by the parameters of his faculties – sight, touch, smell, hearing, and tasting; it is the Soma or carnal realm. The physical body is the medium whereby stimuli enters through the five aforementioned portals into the soulish or natural realm where they are analyzed and processed. It is in this sphere of influence where the consciousness, memory, emotions, affections, imaginations, and reasoning of man is impacted; this is the realm of the psyche. The inner core of man, or the Pneuma or spirit realm, is the dwelling place of the Holy Ghost in the case of those who have been born again.

In order for man to know and understand God, he must move from the physical sphere (the body), through the carnal realm (the soul), into the spiritual realm (the spirit) where God abides. In the days of the tabernacle, the priest had to go through the outer court, through the holy tabernacle, and into the holiest of holies where the Shekinah glory of God would abide.

Many Christians miss the opportunity to experience the fullness of the Spirit. They have been led to believe one of two trends of thought. First, overzealous charismatics have given saints the idea that they must do something to prepare themselves for the baptism in the Holy Spirit. Consequently many individuals have spent an inordinate amount of time "tarrying" for the "baptism." They have literally prayed, fasted, run from one revival to another across the globe seeking a gift that was freely given. Secondly, many Christians simply haven't been taught that the Holy Ghost is for today, or they have been erroneously led to believe that the baptism in the Holy Ghost is not for every Christian. What does the scriptures have to say about these issues?

INTERMINABLE BAPTISM IN THE HOLY GHOST

Dealing with the second issue first, it is important to at least note the theory of Cessationism. Cessationism is a doctrine that in part declares that the gifts of the Holy Ghost and outward expressions of the same are no longer operative or necessary in the contemporary church. Cessastionists deny the authenticity of present day apostles and prophets, and further believe that the gifts of the Spirit, especially speaking in tongues (glossolalia) and prophecy, were only necessary to lay the foundation of the early church. They further contend that since the early Apostles were the foundation of the church, there is no need to continue rebuilding a foundation that has been constructed and sealed. While they do not deny the power of God to perform miracles or to heal, they do not believe that the gifts of miracles or healings are bestowed upon individuals today. Consequently in some denominations, or organizations, there is no expectation of anything beyond conversion and water baptism.

The second chapter in the book of Acts declares in verses 17 and 18, "And it shall come to pass in the last days, saith God, I will pour out of my Spirit (pneuma) upon all flesh; and your sons and your daughters shall prophesy, and your young men shall see visions, and your old men shall dream dreams; And on my servants and on my handmaidens I will pour out in those days of my Spirit (Pneuma), and they shall prophesy." Acts 2:38-39 states, "Then Peter said unto them, Repent, and be baptized, every one of you, in the name of Jesus Christ for the remission of sins, and ye shall receive the gift of the Holy Ghost. For the promise is unto you, and to your children, and to all that are afar off, even as many as the Lord, our God shall call." The Amplified Version of the Bible translates this same passage of scripture as, "And Peter answered them, Repent (change your views and purpose to accept the will of God in your inner selves instead of rejecting it) and be baptized, every one of you, in the name of Jesus Christ for the forgiveness of and release from your sins, and you shall receive the gift of the Holy Spirit. For the promise [of the Holy Spirit] is to and for you and your children, and to and for all that are far away, [even] to and for as many as the Lord our God invites and bids to come to Himself."

There are two points that must be observed in the aforementioned scriptures and translations. First of all, there is an unconditional promise made by God. When God makes a promise, He cannot renege on or rescind it.

> *"For when God made promise to Abraham, because He could swear by no greater, He sware by Himself, saying, surely blessing I will bless thee, and multiplying I will multiply thee. And so, after he had patiently endured, he obtained the promise. For men verily swear by the greater: and an oath for confirmation is to them an end of all strife. Wherein God, willing more abundantly to shew unto the heirs of promise the immutability of His counsel, confirmed it by an oath: That by two immutable*

things, in which it was impossible for God to lie..."
(Hebrews 6:13-18)

In verse 13, God made a promise to the patriarch Abraham and sealed it with an oath in verse 18. Whereas a promise is the verbal or written statement that something will happen or be done, an oath is the affirmation and assurance that the promise will be faithfully performed or executed. It carries with it the collateral of the benefactor and consequences for noncompliance. Oaths are made upon those things that are greater than the promise, yet finite. God who declared that there is nothing greater than Himself and His word, had to swear upon Himself, who is infinite.

It is also clear that when God sets something into motion, He will not change it. The word immutable in verse 18 is translated from the Greek word *amethathetos (am-et-ath`-et-os)*, which literally means that it is not transposed, not to be transferred, fixed, and is unalterable (*Strong's* entry 276). Whatever God releases must be accomplished in its entirety. Heaven and earth would pass away before one iota of God's word can fail. His word is binding and everlasting. Once spoken, it cannot be withdrawn, altered, or dismissed.

The second point that must be considered in Acts 2:38-39 is to whom the promise was directed. While the promise of the baptism in the Holy Ghost was conspicuously manifested on those who were among the 120 individuals gathered together with one accord on the Day of Pentecost, and to other occurrences noted elsewhere in the book of Acts, it is not exclusive to or limited to the generation of the first century church. "For the promise is unto you, and to your children,

Interminable Baptism in the Holy Ghost

and to all that are afar off..." (Acts 2:39) It is evident that this scripture spoke to those who were present when the day of Pentecost was fully come, those in the immediate future, and to distant generations. The only limitation was, "...even as many as the Lord our God shall call." From the date of the initial baptizing in the Holy Ghost, He has not left the church, nor has He withheld Himself from those who will thirst and hunger after Him.

We must remember the sovereignty and faithfulness of God who does not and cannot operate in an arbitrary and capricious manner. In *Finney's Systematic Theology*, Charles Finney (1878) states:

> *"Many seem to me to represent the sovereignty of God as consisting in a perfectly arbitrary disposal of events. They seem to conceive of God as being wholly above and without any law or rule of action guiding His will by His infinite reason and conscience. They appear shocked at the idea of God Himself being the subject of moral law, and are ready to inquire, who gives law to God? They seem never to have considered that God is, and must be, a law unto Himself; that He is necessarily omniscient, and that the divine reason must impose law on, or prescribe law to, the divine will. They seem to regard God as living wholly above law, and as disposed to have His own will at any rate, reasonable or unreasonable; to set up His own arbitrary pleasure as His only rule of action, and to impose this rule upon all His subjects. This sovereignty they seem to conceive of as controlling and disposing of*

all events, with an iron adamantine fatality, inflexible, irresistible, omnipotent." (p. 478)

God does not speak outside of His will and because He alone is sovereign, he must do what He has held Himself to do and perform. God will not violate His own laws or promises. Consequently, the promise of the baptism in the Holy Ghost must be granted according to that which He has released. The scriptures also provide the following guarantee in Numbers 23:19, "God is not a man, that He should lie; neither the son of man, that He should repent: hath He said, and shall He not do it? Or hath He spoken, and shall He not make it good?" It is quite clear that the gift of the baptism in the Holy Ghost is as much for today's believers as it was over two thousand years ago. God will make it good!

Based upon scriptures, the "gift of the Holy Ghost" was not only for the saints of old, but is for every Christian who will receive Him. We must hold to the Word of God and not denomination, -isms, tradition, or anyone else who would try to convince us that the gift of the Spirit was just for the early church. If the Apostles needed this gift in order to operate in power, authority, and anointing, would it not stand to reason that today's believers also need the same baptism? Are you not one of the afar off, the many, the called of God?

In the first Church, the baptism in the Holy Ghost and the gifts of the Spirit were not exclusive to the Apostles, nor to the Jewish converts only. Acts chapter 10 chronicles the account of the Lord's instructions to Peter to go beyond the veil of ethnicity, racism, and tradition to present the gospel of Jesus to Cornelius, a Gentile. After presenting Jesus as the risen Christ to Cornelius' household, an event similar to the Day of Pentecost experience in the upper room took place. "While Peter yet spake these words, the Holy Ghost fell on all them which heard the word. And they of the circumcision which believed were astonished, as many as came with Peter, for they heard them speak with tongues, and magnify God. Then answered Peter, Can any man forbid water, that these should not be baptized, which have received the Holy Ghost as well as we?" (Acts 10:44-47) Once again we see the fulfillment of promise to "…as many as the Lord our God shall call."

THE FREE GIFT OF THE HOLY GHOST

Secondly, we cannot earn the gift of the Holy Ghost any more than we can earn salvation. "For by grace are ye saved through faith; and that not of yourselves, it is the gift of God – Not of works, lest any man should boast." (Ephesians 2:8) There is absolutely nothing you can do to earn the baptism in the Holy Ghost. A gift is freely given, not purchased or earned. One does not merit the gift of the Spirit, nor do we have to necessarily wait on Him. He is freely offered to and readily available to every born again believer. The Word of God is clear on this issue. Every Christian, that is to say every "born again" baptized believer in Jesus Christ, has been qualified by the promise of Jesus and has the right to receive the gift of the Spirit.

Christianity is the only prerequisite to being baptized in the Holy Ghost. God does not and will not put His Spirit (Ruah/Pneuma) in an unclean vessel (sinner). "What? Know ye not that your body is the temple of the Holy Ghost which is in you…" (1 Corinthians 6:19) The believer who has accepted Jesus as Lord and Savior has been washed, purged, sanitized, sanctified (not a denomination), and cleansed by the atoning blood of Christ. 1 John 1:7-9 states, "But if we walk in the light, as He is in the light, we have fellowship one with another, and the blood of Jesus Christ, His Son cleanseth us from all sin. If we say that we have no sin, we deceive ourselves, and the truth is not in us. If we confess our sins, He is faithful and just to forgive us our sins, and to cleanse us from all unrighteousness." The process of regeneration puts the convert in position to not earn, but simply receive the promise of Acts 2:38, "Then Peter said unto them, Repent, and be baptized every one of you in the name of Jesus Christ for the remission of sins, and ye shall receive the *gift* of the Holy Ghost."

According to *Vine's Greek New Testament Dictionary*, the word "gift" in Acts 2:38 is translated from the Greek *dorea*, which denotes a "free gift," stressing its gratuitous character. It is always used in the New Testament as a spiritual or supernatural gift. The clause is epexegetical, the gift being the Holy Ghost Himself. (Vines, 2014) By its very definition a gift cannot be purchased or earned. Meritorious service, good deeds, and religious exercises would all be contradictory to what the Bible clearly categorizes as a gift. As previously mentioned, the immutable nature, words, and promises of God cannot be altered, rescinded, or reneged upon. Once released, they cannot be recalled. Consequently, the process of salvation and faith in the promises of God are all that is necessary to receive that which the Lord has already breathed or released.

Since salvation and the Baptism in the Holy Ghost both come from the same source, God's extension and presentation of them can both be viewed in the context of Ephesians 2:8-9. "For by grace are ye saved through faith; and that not of yourselves: it is the gift of God: Not of works, lest any man should boast." The notion that the Baptism in the

Holy Ghost is anything less than the free gift of God is an egregious error. Consider the case of Simon the Sorcerer who relegated the Holy Spirit to the status of something that could be earned or purchased with money. Simon was so impressed and enamored with the manifest power of the Holy Ghost until, because of selfish and carnal motivation, he wanted to own and manipulate the gift that was freely given. "But Peter said unto him, Thy money perish with thee, because thou hast thought - that the gift of God may be purchased with money." (Acts 8:20) Peter's admonishment and harsh rebuke of Simon cannot be ignored. It also clarifies the gratuitous nature of God who gives that which is far more valuable than the money or services of men. To think that we must merit or provide services or other forms of remuneration is to refute the concept and requirements of faith. "…He that cometh to God must believe that He is, and that He is a rewarder of them that diligently seek Him." (Hebrews 11:6)

CONVERSION OR BAPTISM IN THE SPIRIT

If every saint can be filled with the gift of the Holy Ghost, are there some that have not received the promise? Conversion does not equal or mean baptism in the Holy Spirit. According to the *Scott Foresman Advanced Dictionary*, conversion is defined as follows: 1) a converting; a changing or turning, change; 2) a change from unbelief to faith; changing from one religion to another. It is taken from the Latin word *convertere*. Baptism, on the other hand, is defined as: 1) a rite or sacrament in which a person is dipped in water or sprinkled with water, as a sign of washing away sin and admission into the Christian church. It is taken from the Greek word baptizein, which means to dip. The Greek lexicon defines these words as: Baptizo: 1) to dip repeatedly, to immerse, to submerge; 2) to cleanse by dipping or submerging, to wash, to make clean with water, to wash one's self, to bathe; 3) to overwhelm. Baptizo is also used in the sense of dipping something into dye and to continue dipping until the object is the color (character) of what it is being dipped into. The Greek word for conversion is *epistrophe*, which means conversion of the Gentiles to the one true God.

Although conversion and baptism in the Spirit can happen during the same time period, the conversion must come first. Without a change, an epistrophe, there can be no baptizo. An

Conversion or Baptism in the Spirit

examination of the scriptures will reveal that there were early Christians who were saved (converted) but not filled with the Holy Ghost. In Acts 19:1-7, we find the story of twelve saints in Ephesus who had been saved, epistrophe, but not baptized, baptizo, in the Spirit.

> *"And it came to pass that, while Apollos was at Corinth, Paul having passed through the upper coasts came to Ephesus and, finding certain disciples, he said unto them, have ye received the Holy Ghost since ye believed? And they said unto him, we have not so much as heard whether there is any Holy Ghost. And he said unto them, unto what, then, were ye baptized? And they said, unto John's baptism. Then said Paul, John verily baptized with the baptism of repentance, saying unto the people that they should believe on Him who should come after him, that is, on Christ Jesus. When they heard this, they were baptized in the name of the Lord Jesus. And when Paul had laid his hands upon them, the Holy Ghost came on them, and they spoke with tongues, and prophesied. And all the men were about twelve."*

Ultimately, then, the question is not "Can every Christian be baptized in the Holy Spirit?" The real question is why haven't all saints been baptized in the Spirit? Miseducation, misinterpretation, and a general lack of knowledge regarding what the scriptures declare concerning the gift of the Spirit leads to a forfeiture of the promises of God. "My people are destroyed for a lack of knowledge: because thou hast rejected knowledge, I will also reject thee…" (Hosea 4:6)

When there is a lack of information regarding that which is readily available, people often live life without reaping the benefits of a particular right, privilege, or item. The people of Ephesus did not know to hunger and seek after a greater dimension in God. "We have not so much as heard whether there is any Holy Ghost." Once Paul educated them regarding the person of the Holy Ghost, they were ready to receive the fullness of the Spirit, i.e. the Baptism in the Holy Ghost.

As previously mentioned, the Baptism in the Holy Spirit has been cloaked, shrouded, and obscured by religious doctrine and those in Christendom who failed to fully understand the experiential relationship of God the Holy Ghost. Consequently, many congregations, and members in particular, don't believe that the church can operate in the same dimension of apostolic anointing, power, and authority of the first century church. However, if the issue of being baptized in the Holy Ghost was important enough for the Apostle Paul to ask the saints at Ephesus, is it not equally important today?

NO MORE TARRYING

During the spiritual earthquake known as the Azusa Street Revival that began in April of 1906 under the direction of William Seymour, the Pentecostal movement was birthed. Many of the churches organized as a result of these services believed that it was necessary to emphasize clean, holy, and righteous living. These early Pentecostals also believed that while the Baptism in the Holy Spirit could be instantaneous, it was necessary for the born again believer to wait or "tarry" to receive this gift. At one point, Seymour announced a ten (10) day fast to receive the baptism in the Holy Spirit. (History of the Azusa Street Outpouring, 2014)

It was, and still is, in some denominations, a common practice to conduct tarrying services. These services were designed to tarry, labor, or wait for as long as necessary for a convert to be baptized in the Holy Ghost with the evidence of speaking in tongues (glossolalia). As the name implies, tarrying services can take an extremely large amount of time. While the motivation, intent, and tenacity are quite admirable and well intentioned, the practice is not necessary because the Holy Spirit is here and available to those who will open their hearts. It would also refute the concept of gift of the Holy Spirit, since tarrying would be another process or medium whereby the gift is earned.

Although we don't have to tarry, we must be in a position to receive. Reception can only occur by the faith of the believer and his/her ability and willingness to trust that God will make good on His promise to send another comforter. We must believe that God hears and answers our prayers. Jesus in Mark 9:23 reminds us, "…if thou canst believe, all things are possible to him that believeth." Do you believe?

The gift of the Ruah is not based upon our intellect, emotions, or traditions. The baptism is based upon our knowledge of the truth and the promises of God who cannot lie. We must challenge ourselves to walk by faith and not by sight. Regardless as to how silly, uncomfortable, or different the experience may seem, the gift is ours for the asking and receiving. Resist the temptation to enter into a legalistic struggle. We have a relationship with God who knows how to give good gifts unto His children. Furthermore, we must always adhere to and remember the words of Peter, "…Of a truth I perceive that God is no respecter of persons." (Acts 10:34)

When God sets a spiritual law, promise, or edict into motion, it must perform exactly as He commands. His words will never return void, nor will they return to Him prematurely. They must satisfy every stipulation of the assignment that He releases. In Isaiah 55:11, God proclaimed, "So shall My Word be that goeth forth out of my mouth: it shall not return unto Me void, but it shall accomplish that which I please, and it shall prosper in the thing whereunto I sent it." "The Message" version of Isaiah 55:11 says, "So will the Words that come out of My mouth not come back empty-handed. They'll do the work I sent them to do, they'll complete the assignment I gave them." Every word that God speaks has an assignment. In the case of the promise of the Holy Spirit the assignment was to baptize the believers freely without cost or tarrying. While the time between conversion and baptism in the Holy Ghost undoubtedly varies from Christian to Christian, any tarrying is on the part of the Holy Ghost who is waiting on the believer to simply accept Him by faith. To expect the promise of the Holy Spirit to be given or delivered in a way that is contrary to that which has previously been declared, would be an attempt to cause God to contradict Himself.

THE GIFTS OF THE SPIRIT

As we continue our study of "DE-CLOAKING THE HOLY GHOST," we now turn our attention to the gifts of the Spirit. Jesus promised the disciples that they would receive a spiritual gift from God. In the gospel according to John, Jesus is quoted as saying, "And I will pray the Father, and He shall give you another Comforter, that He may abide with you forever; even the Spirit of truth, whom the world cannot receive because it seeth Him not, neither knoweth Him: but ye know Him; for He dwelleth with you, and shall be in you." (John 14:16 and 17)

Previously we examined and defined the Hebrew word for Spirit. The root word for 'spirit' in Hebrew is 'Ruah' and this word has two distinct meanings. One is 'wind' and the other is 'breath.' One is an impersonal force, the other is a much more intimate, assuming consciousness and awareness. You cannot have breath without having someone who breathes.

In order for the disciples to have the Spirit dwelling inside of them, they had to receive the gift based upon an intimate and personal relationship with Jesus. If we are clear in our understanding that the Holy Spirit is Jesus and God, for all three are one, then we know that it is impossible for Him to dwell in you without causing a change.

The Holy Ruah is active, moving, and imparting. When the Ruah moved upon the face of the waters, dynamic changes

The Gifts of the Spirit

immediately took place. Creation broke out and precious gifts for the use of mankind were immediately deposited in the universe. Gold, diamonds, emeralds, and other precious stones were birthed in the earth. The trees bearing seeds, grains, and other vegetation began to exist. The sea was filled with plankton, fish, and whales. The skies began to be filled with clouds, stars, and birds that could take wing on the wind of the Ruah. GIFTS!!! It should be noted that these gifts were not earned, purchased, or tarried for, but freely given by the designs of God.

Jesus verifies that the Spirit changes and empowers the believer. Luke 14:49 declares, "And behold, I send the promise of my Father upon you; but tarry ye in the city of Jerusalem, until ye be endued with power from on high." Since we know that the Ruah left gifts in the universe, what happens when believers are immersed in Him? To answer this question, we must examine what happened when the promise of the Father was fulfilled.

In Acts chapter 2, we get the answers that inquiring minds want to know: "And when the day of Pentecost was fully come, they were all with one accord in one place. And suddenly there came a sound from heaven like a rushing mighty wind, and it filled all the house where they were sitting. And there appeared unto them cloven tongues as of fire, and it sat upon each of them. And they were all filled with the Holy Ghost, and began to speak with other tongues, as the Spirit gave them utterance."(Acts 2:1-4) Upon receipt of the gift those who were tarrying in Jerusalem received a deposit of gifts. They were forever changed. The power of the Ruah was now inside them. Prior to the crucifixion, the power, Jesus, was on the outside. Even though they were with Him and had a measure of faith, they were limited in what they could do. Now the power was in them and limited only by their faith. Jesus said in Mark 9:23 "…If thou canst believe, all things are possible to him that believeth." The power of the Spirit was now here, forever eliminating the need to tarry for Him. Their wait was over; the power that Christ had promised was fulfilled.

Spiritual gifts were manifested as further evidence of the baptism in the Spirit. Earlier we defined the word baptism as translated from the Greek word baptizo, which means 1) to dip repeatedly, to immerse, to submerge; 2) to cleanse by dipping or submerging, to wash, to make clean with water, to wash one's self, to bathe; 3) Overwhelm (*Strong's*). Those present at the Pentecost fulfillment were immersed, cleansed, washed, bathed, and overwhelmed by the Spirit!

One hundred and twenty people were baptized in the Spirit, which was confirmed and validated by each of them speaking in "other tongues as the Spirit gave them utterance." (Acts 2:4) Each recipient of the baptism in the Holy Ghost spoke in a language that was not their native tongue; a language that previously had been unknown and unlearned by them. There were no fewer than 15 languages being spoken by the Galilean assemblage, as verified by the Jewish diaspora present in the city during the feast of Pentecost. They gave witness declaring that they all heard them speak the wonderful works of God in their native tongues.

While there is a tendency for most people to focus only on the gift of tongues, there are nine Spiritual gifts listed by the Apostle Paul in the book of 1 Corinthians, chapter 12. "For to one is given, by the Spirit, the word of *WISDOM*;

to another, the word of *KNOWLEDGE* by the same Spirit; To another, *FAITH* by the same Spirit; to another, the *GIFTS OF HEALING* by the same Spirit; To another, the *WORKING OF MIRACLES*; to another, *PROPHECY*; to another, *DISCERNING OF SPIRITS*; to another, *VARIOUS KINDS OF TONGUES*; to another, the *INTERPRETATION OF TONGUES.*"

The gifts of the Spirit fall into three major categories:

- Gifts of Inspiration: Tongues, Interpretation of Tongues, Prophecy
- Gifts of Revelation: Word of Wisdom, Word of Knowledge, Discerning of Spirits
- Gifts of Power: Faith, Healings, Miracles

Of the three categories listed above, the gifts of inspiration have probably been the most misunderstood, debated, and controversial. Congregations and denominations have literally split and gone their separate ways over this issue. Is this the will of an omniscient God? Would Jesus promise a gift that would divide His people and set them at odds? The scriptures would offer a resounding NO to these questions. It was Jesus who said, "…If a kingdom be divided against itself, that kingdom cannot stand. And if a house be divided against itself, that house cannot stand. And if satan rise up against himself, and be divided, he cannot stand, but hath an end." (Mark 3:24-26) Although Christ was referring to the impossibility of Himself being empowered by satan in this lesson to the scribes, it would equally apply to the household of faith.

God is a God of order and unity. The gifts of the Holy Spirit were not given to cause division and animosity; they were given to empower the people of God to be more than conquerors. The gifts were given to strengthen, encourage, and to equip the saints for victory throughout the ages. They were also a validation to unbelievers that the hand of God was indeed with the saints, and that they were commissioned by Him to be His representatives and ambassadors on the earth. Carnal minded men and legalists who seek to analyze, define, and approach God through logic and intellect have perverted what should have caused great joy and unity in the household of faith.

In his online Bible Study entitled *Acts 2 – The Holy Spirit Is Poured Out On The Church*, David Guzik (2014) offers the following observations:

"What are we to make of the phenomenon of speaking in tongues? Speaking in tongues has been the focal point for significant controversy in the church. People still ask the same question these bystanders asked on the day of Pentecost.

There is no controversy that God, at least at one time, gave the church the gift of tongues. But much of the controversy centers on the question, 'What is God's purpose for the gifts of tongues?'

Some think that the gift of tongues was given primarily as a sign to unbelievers (1 Corinthians 14:21-22) and as a means to miraculously communicate the gospel in diverse languages. They believe there is no longer the need for this sign so they regard tongues as a gift no longer present in the church today.

Others argue that the gift of tongues, while a sign to unbelievers as stated by 1 Corinthians 14:21-22, are primarily a gift of communication between the believer and God (1 Corinthians 14:2, 13-15), and is a gift still given by God today.

Many mistakenly interpret this incident in Acts 2, assuming that the disciples used tongues to preach to the gathered crowd. But a careful look shows this idea is wrong. Notice what the people heard the disciples say: Speaking…the wonderful works of God. The disciples declared the praises of God, thanking Him with all their might in unknown tongues. The gathered crowd merely overheard what the disciples exuberantly declared to God.

The idea that these disciples communicated to the diverse crowd in tongues is plainly wrong. The crowd had a common language (Greek), and Peter preached a sermon to them in that language! (Acts 2:14-40)" (Guzik, 2014)

The Inspirational Gifts — tongues, interpretation of tongues, and prophecy — were given to edify and strengthen the individual believer and the congregation as a whole. Most of the criticism of those who claim to have been endowed with these gifts is based upon misinformation, intimidation, and sheer misunderstanding.

Why do some Christians believe in the inspirational gifts of the Spirit and others do not? Who is right and who is to blame? Remember, people are quick to attack things that are alien and not part of their life's experiences. We must also consider that many Christians, who believe in the gifts of the Spirit, have also helped to cause confusion and disruption. Some, in their zealousness, have come across as arrogant, offensive, and self-righteous.

Saints in each group have used certain verses of the Bible to batter the other. For example, those who believe in operating in the inspirational gifts will use 1 Thessalonians 5:19, "Quench not the Spirit," to attack those who do not believe in speaking in tongues. Those who believe that these gifts are no longer necessary or present will use 1 Corinthians 13:8, "…Whether there be tongues, they shall cease…"; and 1 Corinthians 14:28, "But if there be no interpreter, let him keep silence in the church…" to support their position. Needless to say, it is imperative that all scriptures be examined in proper scope and context. Failure to examine and rightly divide the Word of Truth inevitably leads to misinformation, misinterpretation, and wrong revelation.

It is quite unfortunate that the people of God are at odds with each other over the promise, purpose, and function of the gifts of the Holy Spirit as it pertains to individual believers in today's world. Rather than tearing down the kingdom of satan, an inordinate amount of time has been spent tearing down the congregations of fellow Christians.

As previously established, the gift of the Holy Ghost is for Christians of every era. That is to say that God is still baptizing saints in the Spirit. Despite controversy and disagreements, people are still speaking in tongues, interpreting tongues, prophesying, receiving words of knowledge and wisdom, discerning spirits, operating in faith, and performing miracles and healings.

WHY THE CONTROVERSY?

For years, theologians, clerics, lay people, and Sunday school students have argued about the gifts of tongues. The anti-tongue groups basically fall into two schools: the strict legalists are they who say, "Nobody should speak in tongues unless an interpreter is present" and the "I don't believe people speak in tongues today. That was just given for one day" (totally unsupported by scripture).

The strict legalists base their philosophy on the instructions that Paul wrote to the church at Corinth. "If any man speak in an unknown tongue, let it be by two, or at the most by three, and that by course; and let one interpret. But if there be no interpreter let him keep silence in the church; and let him speak to himself…" (1 Corinthians 14:27-28) Based upon these verses, they demand the presence of an interpreter. It should be noted that the Corinthian church was extremely dysfunctional and out of order. There were acts of sexual impropriety that were known to exist, yet ignored. The saints had to be admonished not to take each other before secular courts, even in the exercise of spiritual gifts they were given to emotionalism and confusion. People, although blessed with spiritual gifts, were very spiritually immature. In their zealousness they would get caught up in self and in demonstrating their newly received power and failed to edify the entire congregation. Does this mean that Paul was

Why the Controversy?

frowning upon the gifts of the Spirit? Did he ban and prohibit the spiritual gifts? Paul neither frowned upon spiritual gifts and manifestations, nor did he ban and prohibit their use. Paul was simply trying to get the Corinthian congregation to operate in an orderly fashion. His message could be summed up in the expression "there's a time and a place for everything."

If we examine 1 Corinthians 13 and the rest of chapter 14, we will find some interesting facts. First, Paul was a Spirit-filled, tongue-talking Christian and he wanted all saints to share this experience. Consider chapter 13, verse 1, "Though I speak with the tongues of men and of angels…" and 14:18, "I thank my God, I speak with tongues more than ye all." Paul's conversion occurred on the road to Damascus, and his baptism in the Spirit came later in the city of Damascus in the house of Judas (the conversion came first).

As previously mentioned, when the Holy Spirit enters a believer, spiritual gifts are deposited. Paul believed in tongues, spoke in tongues, and never prohibited anyone from speaking in tongues. In fact, he clearly states in I Corinthians 14:5, "I would that ye all spoke with tongues…" He never told the Corinthians to not speak in tongues. Paul simply wanted them to do things decently and in order. He was concerned that people would get caught up in the gift and not in the giver of the gifts. When the congregation should have been intently listening to the sermon, some enthusiastic excited members would speak out loudly at an inopportune time. Does this not happen in our churches now, when people are shouting out so loudly that they drown out the messenger? It is not that what they are saying or doing is wrong; it is simply the wrong time for their oblations. Some of these outbursts are due to a lack of knowledge and understanding, while others are the result of spiritual immaturity.

IT'S TIME TO SET THE RECORD STRAIGHT

Tongue talking is encouraged and permissible in contemporary Christianity! While people often quote a portion of what Paul said regarding the guidelines and restrictions for speaking in tongues, he further stated, "…Forbid not to speak with tongues. Let all things be done decently and in order."(1 Corinthians 14:39 and 40) We must remember that God always has a purpose. Even the creation of man was for His honor and His glory — purpose. Jesus died on the cross to save our souls — purpose. The Holy Ghost was sent to empower and to comfort — purpose. Tongues are given to edify and strengthen the believer — purpose. "For he that speaketh in an unknown tongue speaketh not unto men, but unto God…" (1 Corinthians 14:2)

Speaking in tongues is a divine portal that provides a medium for direct communication that cannot be translated or understood in the physical (soma) or the soulish (psyche) realms; but in the spirit (pneuma) realm wherein is the Holiest of Holies. It is in this gift where deep spiritual thoughts and revelations that cannot be uttered are released to God which edifies the believer. It operates in the faith "sphere" where the physical body and soul status of man is too intimidated to venture. When communication in unknown tongues is interpreted, the Church as well as the individual is edified.

There are basically two categories of tongues: private and public. When tongues are spoken in private, or quietly in the congregation, there is no need for interpretation. The spirit of the believer is speaking directly to God about things that cannot be uttered but by "groanings and moanings." (Romans 8:26) People who are speaking in tongues quietly in the congregation should be no more condemned than the individual who whispers a quiet "Lord have mercy." When the tongues are loud enough to attract the attention of the entire congregation, public tongues, interpretation should be prayed for and sought.

Many who believe in the gifts of tongues have provided ammunition to the critics of this beautiful gift. Individuals who constantly and loudly speak in tongues to the disruption of the order of service, and then make the excuse "I'm so full of the Spirit I can't help myself," are completely out of order and not walking according to the Word of God. In 1 Corinthians 14:32 Paul said, "…the spirits of the prophets are subject to the prophets." He basically is telling the saints that we are in control of the gifts. Although Christians speak in tongues as the Spirit of God gives utterance, they are in control. The Spirit will not make us do anything out of order.

The New Testament contains over thirty references to the gift of tongues. According to John Sherrill in his book, *They Speak With Other Tongues*, there are two very distinct uses for the gift of tongues:

"A sign that the Holy Ghost has entered a certain believer. The tongue seems to have little importance in itself; it is valued only as evidence of something else…The book of Acts, written toward the end of the first century, and which no one has suspected of later additions, refers several times to tongues as a sign of the Holy Spirit's presence. Three things, I thought, were worth noting about these references.

Tongues were accepted as incontestable proof that the Holy Spirit had come upon a given person or group of people...

It was equally uncontested that tongues were the result of the Spirit Himself speaking through men...

The tongues themselves excited very little notice. When Peter was summing up his experience in Caesarea for the church in Jerusalem, he didn't bother to mention tongues at all, although they had been a salient part of the happening there;

2) So far, tongues have been treated as a sign of the Holy Spirit's coming. But when I turned to Paul's letters, it was obvious that he was looking at them very differently. Paul was discussing tongues, not as a one-time outpouring, but as a continuing experience. They were a gift of the Spirit for the advantage of the believer, to be used along with the eight other gifts for the up building of God's people." (Sherrill 1985)

According to Sherrill, in Paul's view there seemed to be three principle ways in which tongues were of value. First, in private prayer, tongues aided the speaker to praise God. When the believer speaks to God in a heavenly language, inhibitions and logical intellectual dependence is shattered by the anointing of the Holy Spirit. Consequently, the believer is released to offer unbridled passionate praises to Jehovah-God. When Christians are empowered by the Holy Ghost to speak in tongues, societal and cultural restraints are shattered and removed because the Spirit of God ushers in liberty.

It's Time to Set the Record Straight

Consequently, the innermost court of the triune man is exposed and open to the sensitivity of the Holy Spirit. When the veil of the temple, or in this case the human tabernacle, is breached, the entrance and glory of God is accessible.

Secondly, speaking in tongues allows the believer to pray, even in those times when he/she is not sure of what to submit to God. Confusion, stress, and the weight of life's burdens can cripple and cause us to be so heavy in our body (soma) and soul (psyche) until we don't truly know where to begin in trying to explain our position and request to God who is able and ready to honor our appeal. It is in the spirit realm (pneuma) in which we utter those things that cannot be understood in the intellectual or natural realm of man. Speaking in tongues solidifies our spiritual connection to Jehovah-Jireh, who searches the hearts and reigns of man and Who alone knows and understand what it is that we need to communicate. The impact in the spirit realm is released and flooded into the soulish realm; subsequently, there is a manifestation in the physical realm. "And this is the confidence that we have in Him, that, if we ask any thing according to His will, He heareth us: And if we know that He hear us, whatsoever we ask, we know that we have the petitions that we desired of Him." (1 John 5:14-15)

Thirdly, speaking in tongues during public worship, when accompanied by another of the nine gifts, interpretation, provides a vehicle of direct communication between God and man. The interpreted tongue provides edification from the mouth of God to His children. When public tongues are interpreted, a prophetic word is often released to the entire congregation. Admonishment, correction, and exhortation can be released when speaking publicly in tongues is properly administered. Public tongues also serves notice to nonbelievers that the Holy Ghost does indeed inhabit those who have opened themselves up to His presence and gifting. The interpretation of tongues validates the individual being used by God and the entire congregation. It is a means whereby the power and presence of God is manifested and experienced by the corporate body; an outward declaration to all in attendance that He yet abides with His children.

DO THEY ALL SPEAK WITH TONGUES?

Does everyone who receives the baptism in the Holy Ghost speak in tongues? Although this is the opinion of many Pentecostal saints, it is unlikely that scriptures can support such a case. The book of Acts records five incidents in which people were baptized in the Holy Ghost. In three of those five occasions, people speaking in other tongues evidenced the baptism. In the other two it can be assumed that tongue talking may have been present. One involved Paul in the house of Ananias. Although the book of Acts does not clearly state that Paul spoke in tongues when he was filled with the Spirit, Paul did confirm in the book of Corinthians that he had the gift of tongues. (1 Corinthians 14:18)

The other incident in which tongue talking was not clearly stated occurred in Acts chapter 8. Philip had preached a tremendous message in the city of Samaria. As a result many people were converted and baptized in water. When the Apostles who were at Jerusalem heard that Samaria had received the word of God, they sent Peter and John to finish the work started by Philip. Peter and John laid hands on the people of Samaria and prayed for them to receive the gift of the Holy Ghost and they were filled. Simon the Sorcerer, one of Philip's converts, was absolutely astonished by whatever happened when the people received the Holy Ghost. In fact, the scriptures record that he tried to buy the gift of being able to lay hands on people and filling them with the Spirit. Although he was sorely reprimanded, can we conclude that his enthusiasm was generated by people speaking in tongues? There had to have been some manifestation or sign that the people had been filled with the Spirit. Why else would Simon offer money to possess such power?

Sherrill offers the following answer to the question, "Does everyone who receives the Holy Spirit speak in tongues, and that if you have not spoken in tongues you have not really received the Holy Spirit?" "I do not believe that you can make such a case from Scripture. However, the book of Acts suggests to us a helpful pattern: 1) Receiving the Holy Spirit is a definite, clear cut, instantaneous experience; 2) A simple and God-appointed way for you objectively to manifest the gift of the Holy Spirit is to lift up your voice in faith, and speak out in a new tongue at the prompting of the Holy Spirit." (Sherrill, 1985)

The writer seems to adhere to the view that there is no scriptural support for the notion that tongues are the only sign that individuals have been filled with the Spirit. We must remember that there are eight other gifts of the Spirit.

Paul, in addition to having the gift of tongues, also possessed the gift of prophecy, and was used in the gift of healing. He admonished the saints to desire the gift of prophecy because it edified the entire congregation. Some will contend that prophecy is a greater gift because of this statement. However, Paul simply said in 1 Corinthians 14:5, "I would that ye all spoke with tongues, but rather that ye prophesied; for greater is he that prophesieth than he that speaketh with tongues, except he interpret, that the church may receive edifying." We must not view the gift of tongues as some sort of inferior or weak gift from God. God's gifts are always superior. Tongues, to a large degree, tend to be individual in nature and without interpretation will not edify those who are listening.

Don Basham (1971) in his book, *Tongues, Interpretation, And Prophecy*, states, "It needs to be understood that Paul is not exalting one spiritual gift above another, but merely placing priority on the gifts which edify the church because he was writing about a church problem, not about an individual problem. In the assembled congregation, Paul says prophecy is of a greater value than tongues since all those hearing the prophecy can understand the meaning of what is said."

All of the gifts must be used decently and in order. Because God is not an author of confusion, everything He does and gives must be systematic and coherent. He never does anything that is chaotic, but brings order and procedure out of chaos. In the book of Genesis we discover the meticulous, methodical nature of God. He does not make man until he restores order to the earth. Had God haphazardly created man during His work on the first five days of creation, man would not have survived. He waited until day six when everything was in order and prepared to receive the centerpiece of His work. Likewise, it is inconceivable that God would send His Spirit bearing gifts to cause chaos and confusion within the Household of Faith. That would be to simulate the earth mentioned in Genesis 1:2, "And the earth was without form, and void; and darkness was upon the face of the deep…"

The Holy Spirit brings order, form, fullness, and light into situations that are formless, void, and dark.

Regarding prophecy, Paul said, "Let the prophets speak two or three, and let the others judge. If anything be revealed to another that sitteth by, let the first hold his peace. For ye may all prophesy one by one, that all may learn, and all may be comforted." (1 Corinthians 14:29-31) Notice how relentless Paul is when it comes to uplifting the body of Christ. Individuals who claim to have the gift of prophecy must be careful to speak only those things that have been given to them by the Holy Spirit. While prophecy may contain rebuke, correction, and instruction it should never be doom and gloom. Many people have been coerced, intimidated, and manipulated by people who claim to be prophets.

What is prophecy? "Prophecy is a supernatural gift. It is speaking forth by direct inspiration of the Holy Spirit the words of God to His people. It is not merely inspirational or eloquent speaking…" (Basham, 1971) God's prophets are not *Psychic Friends!* Prophecy is more forth-telling the mind and heart of God than it is foretelling, although it can contain both aspects. Foretelling is predictive in nature and content, declaring the will of God and His plans for His people. Forth-telling deals with the application of revealed truths as it relates to current situations and circumstances. It is generally a call to repentance and a reminder of the veracity and immutability of what God has already spoken.

Prophecy must contain three elements: edification, exhortation, and comfort. "But he that prophesieth speaketh unto men to edification, and exhortation, and comfort." (1

Corinthians 14:3) The definitions for edification, exhortation, and comfort are as follows:

> Edification – moral improvement; spiritual benefit; instruction; to uplift. It is translated from the Greek Oikodome {oy-kod-om-ay} which is the act of one who promotes another's growth in Christian, wisdom, piety, happiness and holiness. (*Strong's*, 2001)
>
> Exhortation – strong urging; earnest advice or warning. In the Greek, exhortation from the word Paraklesis {par-ak-lay-sis}, means a calling or summons for help, it affords encouragement and refreshing. It is a persuasive discourse that is stirring, instructive, and admonitory in nature. (*Strong's*, 2001)
>
> Comfort – ease the grief or sorrow; anything that makes trouble or sorrow easier to bear; consolation. Paramuthia {par-am-oo-thee`-ah} in the Greek is translated to the English word comfort which is any address, whether made for the purpose of persuading, or of arousing and stimulating, or of calming and consoling. (*Strong's*, 2001)

Prophecy is not God gossiping and telling the innermost secrets of one person to others for the purpose of public broadcasting. While prophecy may be used to convict as well as for confirmation, it must never be used as a means to control or batter another person. In all matters of prophecy, we must consult God for the final word and not some well-meaning individual. Remember "…the spirits of the prophets are subject to the prophets."

Far too often the sheep of the kingdom have been damaged by "Parking lot and Bathroom Prophets," individuals who prophesy for personal gain and glory. When a misplaced word or word out of season is given to a believer who may not be well rooted or studied in the scriptures, the potential for great harm and disaster is very possible. Unfortunately, we are in a time in which many people for a plethora of reasons are clamoring after and seeking signs and wonders. While ministries should be validated by the hand of God and the manifestations of signs and wonders, we are never encouraged to seek after mystical events that may be truly amazing but not necessarily a genuine move of God. In the gospel according to Matthew 16:4, Jesus declared, "A wicked and adulterous generation seeketh after a sign; and there shall no sign be given unto it, but the sign of the prophet Jonas…" We must remain cognizant of the fact that satan has always attempted to challenge or counterfeit everything God created. In the Garden of Eden, satan challenged the veracity and faithfulness of God's Word by declaring to the woman that she and Adam would not die if they ate fruit from the forbidden tree. Whereas God told Adam that he would surely die, satan told Eve that they would not die because they would be on an equal footing with God. (Genesis 3:4-5) In the New Testament, Paul warned the body of Christ to not be mesmerized by sensationalism or those things that appeared to be miraculous, because satan is a master of illusion. Paul was keenly aware of satan's ability to pervert truth and to forge his own brand of miracles. (1 Corinthians 11:13-15)

Unfortunately, many overzealous saints fail to understand that faith does not have to seek after signs and wonders because signs and wonders are assigned to follow faith. "And these signs shall follow them that believe…" (Mark 16:17)

THE GIFTS OF THE SPIRIT

Previously we established several points. First, the Holy Ghost is not a what, or an it. The Spirit is a who, a He, the third person in the Triune God. The Holy Spirit is as much God as any of the other two persons of the Godhead. The personality of the Spirit and His operations are clearly established and defined throughout the scriptures.

We further established the fact that the Holy Ghost is a gift from God. He cannot be purchased or earned. We cannot receive this blessed gift through our intellect, merit, or good deeds. We must receive the gift of the Spirit by faith. Furthermore, we verified that the gift of the Spirit is for today. The nine spiritual gifts enumerated in 1 Corinthians chapter 12 are yet functioning in today's believing and receiving Christians.

Finally we discovered, through scriptures, that Christianity is the only prerequisite to being baptized in the Spirit. It has nothing to do with what denomination one might belong, or how long a person has been saved. It is not predicated upon the value or worth of a believer, but like salvation, this gift is free.

The scriptures also point out that conversion and the baptism of the Spirit does not always occur simultaneously. In fact, the conversion must take place first. These two experiences are separate and distinct. The book of Acts chronicles a number of occasions in which born again believers in Christ received the baptism in the Holy Ghost some time after their conversion.

The Gifts of the Spirit

As stated previously, there were nine gifts of the Spirit as enumerated by the Apostle Paul (1 Corinthians 12:8-9). The gifts were divided into three categories 1) Inspirational Gifts – tongues, interpretation of tongues, and prophecy; 2) Revelation Gifts – word of knowledge, word of wisdom, and discerning of spirits; and 3) Gifts of Power – faith, healings, and miracles.

Thus we have examined the gifts that have been the center of controversy throughout church history, the Inspirational Gifts. We concluded that there are basically two types of tongues, Private and Public. We also focused on the appropriate use and order for speaking in tongues. Speaking in tongues is for today's saints! Although many well-meaning Christians have tried to use Apostle Paul's teachings in the book of 1 Corinthians to banish the gift of tongues, Paul took the opposite position. He encouraged speaking in tongues. In fact, he spoke in tongues on a frequent basis. Paul was simply trying to teach the dysfunctional Corinthian church to do things decently and in order.

Although we have already discussed to some degree the inspirational gift of speaking in tongues, or glossolalia, we will continue to examine this gift and the benefits of being baptized in the Holy Ghost. Remember the Greek lexicon defines baptizo as: to dip repeatedly, to immerse, and to submerge. It means to cleanse by submerging. And finally, the word baptizo means to overwhelm. Earlier we discovered that when the Spirit moved upon the face of the earth, great things happened. The Spirit also made deposits in the air, water, and land. In fact, when the Spirit moved in the lifeless lump of clay that was made in the image and likeness of God, man received a deposit and became a living soul. Likewise, when the Spirit immerses, submerges, and overwhelms a believer, his/her character is changed and spiritual gifts are deposited.

Although, we do not espouse the belief that speaking in tongues (glossolalia) is the only evidence that someone has been baptized in the Spirit, we do believe that an obvious manifestation will take place. Throughout the scriptures we find a common trait amongst those who have been in the direct presence of God. They were all permanently changed.

At 80 years of age, and a fugitive from the Egyptian judicial system, Moses became God's pastor of the wilderness assembly. He boldly confronted Pharaoh and told him to let God's people go! When Samuel was but a child, he heard the voice of God calling him and became one of God's greatest prophets. Jeremiah described his personal encounter with God as fire shut up in his bones. In Psalms 107:2, David said, "Let the redeemed of the Lord say so." There is no baptism without some type of evidence. Even when we are baptized in water, there is evidence that we have been immersed. How much more, then, should there be evidence of a spiritual baptism?

When we examine the gifts of the Spirit, we notice a characteristic that is common among them all. Each gift, when used in love, serves to edify. Speaking in tongues edifies the individual believer, and when accompanied by interpretation, edifies the entire congregation. As mentioned heretofore, there are two types of tongues, Private and Public.

The following information was obtained from a Bible study presented at the new Christian Valley Full Gospel Church in Chicago, Illinois, where a friend of this author, Apostle H. Daniel Wilson is the pastor (Wilson, 2000).

SPEAKING IN TONGUES
Separate Experiences Can Happen at the Same Time

Personal	*Public*
1) Private devotion Prayer life (1 Corinthians 14:18)	1) Tongues along with interpretation is equivalent to prophecy (1 Corinthians 14:5)
2) Tongues may be spoken privately and God gives the individual interpretation for his own edification (1 Corinthians 14:14, 15)	2) Personal tongues as a form of prayer may be spoken in public as long as it's done decent and in order (Mark 16:17-18, 1 Corinthians 14:37-40)
3) Spirit to spirit. God's Spirit in you talking and praising and communicating to Himself (1 Corinthians14:2; 14; Ephesians 6:18, Romans 8:26)	3) Tongues can be spoken in public without an interpreter as long as it is not glaring, disruptive, or out of order. There is time, during public worship where tongues may go forth during corporate prayer or praise and worship (1 Corinthians 14:12-13, 20-22)
4) Tongues is a prayer which edifies (builds-up) the believers (1 Corinthians 14:4, Jude 20; Romans 14:19; Ephesians 4:24; 29)	4) When tongues go forth in public, and it is glaring, exceeding normal current word level of the service, one should begin to pray for interpretation; for there should be a message in this tongue for the whole church; or the individual should be silent (1 Corinthians 14:12-13, 14:5)
5) Spiritually refreshing (Isaiah 28:11-12)	

Salvation	*Baptism in the Spirit*
Changes your position with God (from sinner to saint) Christ in the person of The Holy Spirit enters into the believer	Endowment of power from on high
1) Romans 10:9-10, Believe in thine heart.	1) Acts 2:4. The 120 on the day of Pentecost were already believers and received this in addition to salvation
2) Acts 4:12. No other name given.	2) The Samaritans: saved under Philip's ministry received the Holy Spirit when Peter and John laid hands on them. (Acts 8:5-17)
3) John 14:6. I am the truth	3) Ananias laid hands on Paul and he received the Holy Spirit (Acts 9:3-18)
4) Romans 1:16. I am not ashamed of the gospel for it is the power of salvation to everyone that believes	4) Cornelius years after the day of Pentecost; first gentile converts (Acts 11:14) filled with the Holy Spirit and spoke with tongues (Acts 10:44-46)
5) Mark 16:15-16, "…Go ye into all the world, and preach the gospel to every creature. He that believeth and is baptized shall be saved…"	5) The Ephesian disciples were saved and had been baptized. When Paul laid hands on them, they were filled with the Holy Spirit (Acts 19:1-7)

Ten Reasons Why Every Believer Should Desire to Speak in Tongues

1. The Word teaches that when we are filled with the Holy Ghost, we speak with other tongues as the Spirit of God gives utterance. (Acts 2:4; 10:46)
2. God through the Apostle Paul encouraged the Corinthian church to continue the practice of speaking in tongues and never rescinded that encouragement. He also encouraged them to speak in tongues in their individual prayer lives as a means of spiritual edification or building up. (1 Corinthians 14:14; Jude 20)
3. Speaking in tongues keeps us continually aware of the Holy Spirit's indwelling presence.
4. Speaking in tongues eliminates the possibility of selfishness entering our prayer life. (Romans 8:26)
5. Believers should desire to speak in tongues for it helps them learn to trust God more. (Jude 20; Proverbs 3:5)
6. Speaking in tongues is a means of keeping us free from contamination of the ungodly and profane elements of the world. (1 Corinthians 14:2) You can pray in tongues to yourself.
7. The believer should desire to speak in tongues because it provides a way for things to be prayed for which no one thinks to pray about.
8. A very good reason to speak in tongues is the refreshing and rest that comes with it. (1 Corinthians 14:21; Isaiah 28:11-12)

9. As believers we have been commanded to give thanks for all things. Speaking in tongues is a way to give thanks. (1 Corinthians 14:15-17)
10. The tenth reason why every believer should desire to speak with tongues is found in James 3:8, "But the tongue can no man tame; it is an unruly evil full of deadly poison." Yielding your tongue to the Holy Spirit to speak with other tongues is a big step toward being able to fully yield all of your members to God. For if you can yield your tongue, you can yield any member of your body to God. (Romans 12:1)

The gift of speaking tongues liberates the believer and moves him/her beyond the limitations of the natural realm into a sphere of edification that impacts more than the conscious self. Speaking in tongues moves the recipient beyond the threshold of the outer court of man (body/soma), through the inner court (soul/psyche), into the most holy place (spirit/pneuma) or core of who he is. It is only in the Spirit that we can worship the Father. (John 4:23)

When the gift of speaking in tongues is in operation, a direct line of communications is made between the spirit of man and the Holy Spirit. Because the Spirit always brings and or restores liberty, the natural inhibitions and fears of the believer are allayed. Consequently, there is a freedom to express the inner most suppressed thoughts of the spirit man with language that cannot be otherwise verbalized. "Likewise the Spirit also helpeth our infirmities: for we know not what we should pray for as we ought: but the Spirit itself maketh intercession for us with groanings which cannot be uttered." (Romans 8:26) Speaking with tongues is how that supernatural power is released into our lives. If we do not speak with tongues, that power is never released. (Price, 1996)

THE GIFT OF TONGUES

In the book of 1 Corinthians 12, the Apostle Paul seems to differentiate between the tongues experienced and manifested in the book of Acts and the gift of divers tongues mentioned in 1 Corinthians 12:10. In Acts, the Word of God declares that they spoke with "other tongues" as the Spirit gave them utterance. There are at least three (3) concrete illustrations and two (2) that are inferred, in which people spoke with other tongues as a result of having been baptized with the Holy Spirit. (Acts 2:4, 14-21; 9:17-18; 10:44-47; 19:1-6) Other tongues refer to languages other than the native or learned tongue of the believer. Again, these tongues may be public or private but can only edify the corporate body when properly translated. The distinguishing characteristic between other tongues and the gift of divers tongues is twofold in nature. One serves as evidence that one has been baptized in the Holy Spirit, while the other is a gift given by the Spirit with somewhat differences in administration. Consider the following excerpt taken from Dr. Frederick K. C. Price's book, (1996) *"The Holy Spirit. The Helper We All Need"*:

> *"The gifts of the Spirit are not for everyone in the Body of Christ. They are actually for the ministry gifts God places in the Church. Nevertheless, every person in the Body of Christ who is filled with the Spirit may*

on occasion be used by the Spirit in any one of the manifestations of those nine gifts.

Speaking with tongues, on the other hand, is for your personal spiritual enrichment. It does not need an interpretation like the gift of tongues does, because it is simply you speaking to God. An easy way to remember the difference between speaking with tongues and the gift of tongues is that speaking with tongues is man talking to God; it goes from earth to heaven. The gift of tongues, on the other hand, comes from heaven to earth, because it is God speaking through a man to men." (pp. 77-78)

THE GIFT OF INTERPRETATION

As previously mentioned, God is a God of order. He is meticulous in details, systematic in operation, and succinct in purpose. Consequently, it is theologically inconceivable that He would bestow the gift of tongues or speaking in an angelic or heavenly language without providing a method for the corporate body to be edified and equipped by its use. It would stand to reason that if the ascension (or fivefold ministry) gifts were given to perfect the saints to edify the body of Christ (Ephesians 4:11-12) that God, the benefactor, would make clear provisions for understanding precisely what it is that He is conveying to the assembly.

It is imperative that we understand that there is a difference between translation and interpretation. Translation is the process by which the words of one language are presented in the form of another language exactly and precisely as they are delivered. Interpretation on the other hand, is an explanation as to what is being said. Interpretation brings meaning and understanding to what the message is conveying.

The author has had the opportunity to minister and teach the Word of God in several foreign nations and subgroups of differing dialects in the aforementioned nations. During those meetings and lectures, there were times in which it became necessary for the translators to become interpreters because there were no words in the languages of the listeners that had an English equivalent. During a crusade in Soroti, Uganda, an interpreter took a great amount of time interpreting something that was spoken through a few English words. After the crusade, the translator explained that there were no words or phrases in the native tongues of the Ugandan assembly that conveyed the thoughts of the speaker. Consequently, it became necessary at that point to become an interpreter. There are some things that can only be known and made manifest in the spirit realm by the Spirit. It is the purpose of those who operate in the gift of interpretation to provide the meaning of what is being audibly and noticeably spoken by someone operating in the gift of tongues, not by their own summations and opinions, but as deciphered by the Holy Spirit.

There are times when the interpretation in tongues can be predictive, encouraging, instructing, and comforting to the body of Christ. It can bring direction and unity, as well as clarity to a congregation of believers. The gift of tongues should always be accompanied by its companion gift, the gift of interpretation. If there is no interpreter present, the benefits to the body are lost. (1 Corinthians 14:27-28) "The gift of tongues is for public assembly, and should always be accompanied by the companion gift interpretation of tongues. The rare exception to this is when God speaks to an individual through the person doing the speaking. In other words, one person will speak with the gift of tongues, but to the person to whom the message is addressed, it will be in a language he or she will understand." (Price, 1996)

THE GIFT OF PROPHECY

According to *Strong's Exhaustive Concordance of The Bible*, prophecy, from the Greek word Propheteia {prof-ay-ti`-ah}, is a discourse emanating from divine inspiration and declaring the purposes of God, whether by reproving and admonishing the wicked, or comforting the afflicted, or revealing things hidden. As stated earlier, prophecy can be both foretelling and forth-telling. While there are those who would contend that there are no modern day prophets, the Word of God clearly enumerates prophecy as one of the gifts of the Spirit. Having thus said, because a person received a prophetic word does not necessarily affirm that he or she is a prophet, the gifts of the Spirit are not necessarily owned by the believer, but bestowed upon them at the discretion of God the Holy Ghost.

Not unlike the gift of speaking in tongues, prophecy has had its share of controversy and skepticism. To the Cessastionist, this gift is no longer needed as the scriptures have all been canonized and sealed. Their contention is that there is and will be no new revelation. While it is clear that God is not adding to the scriptures, a prophetic word given to someone operating in the gift of prophecy will always correlate with and support the Word of God as it is. Consequently, every word must line up with the Spirit of what God has already spoken. While there is no new revelation, there are times when a revelation will be new to the listener. The 12 Ephesian believers had not heard or had a revelation that there was a Holy Ghost. After Paul brought to them revelation that was new to their ears, they were baptized in the Holy Ghost and spoke in tongues and prophesied. (Acts 19:1-7)

According to Basham, prophecy is a supernatural gift. It is speaking forth by direct inspiration of the Holy Spirit the words of God to His people. It is not merely inspirational or eloquent speaking (p. 102). The prophetic word adds insight to those things that have already been spoken of in the Word of God. While the gift of prophecy may be more forthtelling in nature, it is not prevented from being foretelling. We must remember that God is omniscient and, therefore, knows the end from the beginning (Isaiah 46:10). By His own sovereignty and election, He can share future events with His children. The gift of prophecy may involve warnings or admonishments to a believer or the body general.

Like all gifts, it is imperative that believers develop a spiritually mature understanding and application of the prophetic. Where there is a lack of training and understanding, abuse, misuse, and misunderstanding ensues. This conundrum can be birthed on the part of the one operating in the gift of prophecy as well as those to whom the prophecy is given. Immature Christians are quick to run and operate on a "prophetic" word rather than seeking the wise counsel of God or those who have been spiritually and strategically placed to watch for their souls. Spiritual development and maturity is needed to maintain the decency and order required by the Word of God. (1 Corinthians 14:40) When people operate without constraint and protocol, anarchy prevails under the premise of, "the Spirit made me do it." Guidelines, instructions, and order are not anathema to the concept of permitting the Holy Spirit free course. It is prudent and necessary to judge every prophetic word. "Let the prophets speak two or three, and let the other judge. If any thing be revealed to another that sitteth by, let the first hold his peace. For ye may all prophesy one by one, that all may learn, and all may be comforted. And the spirits of the prophets are subject to the prophets." (1 Corinthians 14:29-32)

There are times when the gift of prophecy serves as confirmation to that which was previously spoken by God. In Peter's prophetic vision on the rooftop, he is instructed by God to slay and eat that which was considered to be common or unclean to Jewish people. Peter responded in the negative, standing on religious custom and Jewish law. Three times a voice speaks to him and encourages him to not judge or condemn that which God cleanses. Prior to Peter's vision, Cornelius, a devout Gentile, has a vision and is instructed by the angel of God to send for Peter. He does not know Peter, Peter does not know him, but yet they have two interconnected visions that are prophetic in nature, in this case foretelling. Peter's vision is not clarified until he obeys the Word of the Lord who had already told him to not condemn that which He cleansed. Now the words are confirmed when Peter and Cornelius meet and share their experiences. It should be noted that it was unlawful for Peter who was a Jew to keep company with a Gentile (Acts 10:28) because Gentiles were "unclean." The vision and the prophetic nature of it simply confirmed the words of the Great Commission (Matthew 28:19), to teach all nations, which obviously would include Cornelius the Gentile.

The Gift of Prophecy

We must be careful to not confuse fortune tellers, soothsayers, astrologers, and spiritual mediums with those who operate in the gift of prophecy. Anyone who seeks personal gain, whether monetary or through notoriety, is sorely out of the will of God and is in a state of rebellion or an agent of satan. While the gift of prophecy is a genuine endowment of the Holy Spirit, Basham offers this warning. "It should be remembered that there is nothing uniquely Christian about predicting the future. Seers, mystics and clairvoyants have been common throughout history, and many of them have amassed a formidable record of success, while having nothing whatever to do with the Christian faith. Such abilities are, of course, of psychic and demonic in origin and are not to be confused with the true gift of prophecy springing from the Holy Spirit through the grace of Jesus Christ." (p. 106)

THE GIFT OF WISDOM

The gift of wisdom exceeds the boundaries of that which can be obtained through the discipline of earthly studies. In order for it to be a gift of the Holy Ghost, it must also surpass the peripheries of human experiences or the lessons of life. In other words, the gift of wisdom cannot be learned, earned, or purchased by the efforts of humanity. Paul's use of the word wisdom in 1 Corinthians 12:8 is translated from the Greek word Sophia {sof-ee`-ah} which deals with supreme intelligence such as belongs to God. It is the wisdom of God as evinced in forming and executing counsels. Sophia denotes a mental excellence of the highest sense. (*Strong's Concordance of the Bible,* 2001)

The gift of wisdom recognizes the logic of the physical realm, yet draws its direction from that which is spiritual. It is the wisdom of this world that is subject to the intellect of humanity and framed by its limitations, biases, and inadequacies. The gift of wisdom has its strength and origins in the counsel of God.

Joseph's ability to interpret dreams is well documented in the book of Genesis chapters 40 and 41. Through the divine guidance of the Holy Spirit, he accurately interpreted the prophetic dreams of the butler and the baker. Joseph declared, or foretold, that in three days the butler would be restored, but the baker would be executed. Although forgotten by the

The Gift of Wisdom

butler, the spiritual gifts operating in Joseph were once again called upon, this time by Pharaoh. It is in the interpretation of Pharaoh's dream that we clearly see the need for divine wisdom. It was one thing for Pharaoh to know what his dreams meant (Genesis 41). It was another thing to know what do with that information. Through wisdom, Joseph provided Godly counsel to Pharaoh, and advised him to store up an abundant amount of grain in the years of abundance that ultimately saved Egypt and Israel during the years of great famine.

The gift of wisdom provides direction and instructions to the body of Christ for growth, development, governance, and understanding in spiritual matters. It equips the saints in their ability to present a compelling case for accepting Jesus to those who are outside of the ark of safety.

The gift of wisdom equips the body of Christ to provide structure as well as order within local congregations. When matters of contention arise in the body of Christ, it is wisdom that is needed rather than debate and schism. During the early days of the Church, the Apostles were criticized by the Grecians for not properly seeing to the needs of the widows who were a part of the congregation. Rather than allowing a fracture to continue developing within the body of Christ, they instructed the multitude to find seven men who were filled with the Holy Ghost and who were blessed with wisdom (Acts 6:3) The word wisdom in this verse comes from the same Greek word that is used in 1 Corinthians 12:8 (Sophia). It would be safe to conjecture that these seven men were endowed with the gift of wisdom.

THE WORD OF KNOWLEDGE

What many erroneously call a word of prophecy is actually a word of knowledge. It is the word of knowledge that empowers the person operating in that gift to know something they previously did not know. This can be information about another individual or group that the Holy Ghost uses to convict, encourage, or instruct. It was Nathan the prophet who had a word of knowledge regarding David's illicit affair with Bathsheba. Nathan used that knowledge to bring the king to conviction and repentance. (2 Samuel 12)

Peter received a word of knowledge regarding Ananias and Sapphira and their conspiracy to lie to the Holy Ghost. This revelation not only resulted in the deaths of these co-conspirators, but it caused great fear to fall upon all the Church, and upon as many as heard these things. (Acts 5:1-11)

Jesus used a word of knowledge to prove to Nathanael that He is indeed the son of God. It was Nathanael who was skeptical of Philip's assertion that Jesus was the Messiah spoken of by Moses in the law. It was Nathanael's contention that nothing good could possibly come out of Nazareth. Nathanael had never met Jesus, but based upon the report that Jesus was from Nazareth, his mind was already made up. When Jesus met him face-to-face and exposed his religious, legalistic, and hypocritical nature, Nathanael did not defend himself, but rather wanted to know how Jesus knew so much about him. Jesus, through the word of knowledge, simply revealed something that no one could have known except Nathanael. "…Before that Philip called thee, when thou wast under the fig tree, I saw thee." Immediately Nathanael's doubts and skepticisms were dismissed. (John 1:45-50)

In 1 Corinthians 12:8, the word *"word"* is translated from Logos {log`-os} meaning to be uttered by a living voice to convey an idea or the sayings of God. Knowledge, on the other hand, comes from Gnosis {gno`-sis}, which means to signify understanding. Rodney W. Francis states, "The Word of Knowledge, therefore, is knowledge received from the Holy Spirit to enable us to more effectively minister to the needs of people, to know and understand situations, circumstances, strategies of the enemy (kingdoms of darkness), etc. It enables us to know how to speak in the above situations with knowledge that can surprise, baffle, disarm, open-up, bring answers, healing, and understanding." (*The Word of Knowledge*, 2014)

The gift of knowledge provides insight into the deeper truths of the scriptures without altering, perverting, or deviating from what has already been spoken by God. This gift allows the beneficiary to go beyond the surface of what a scripture says and reveal what it is saying. In the book of Acts, there is an account of an Ethiopian eunuch who had traveled to Jerusalem to worship. Although he held Old Testament scriptures in his hands and read from the prophet Isaiah, it took Philip to expose the truths of what Isaiah was saying. Philip's gift of knowledge allowed him to use the Word of God, as spoken through Isaiah, to reveal Jesus as the resurrected savior to the Ethiopian eunuch. While they both read from the same passage of scriptures, it is clear that the word of knowledge gave Philip a greater insight and understanding into what the scriptures were saying. As a result of Philip yielding to the power of the Holy Spirit, the Ethiopian eunuch gave his life to Christ and was baptized. (Acts 8:27-40)

THE GIFT OF DISCERNING SPIRITS

The gift of discerning spirits endows the believer with the ability to distinguish and determine what spiritual forces are at work or influential in given situations. It is the ability to accurately perceive the motives behind a particular behavior. Discernment is the quality of being able to grasp and comprehend what is obscure. (Meriam-Webster, 2014) In the New Testament, it is translated from the Greek word Diakrisis {dee-ak`-ree-sis}, meaning to distinguish, differentiate, and pass judgment.

The gift of discernment differs from discernment that comes about as a result of spiritual maturity. Individuals who have grown beyond the basic fundamentals of Christianity and who have endured spiritual battles in the process of living have had plenty of experiences to grow and mature in Christ. As a result of being stretched in their faith and proven by fiery trials, they have learned to feed on a spiritual diet of strong meat. Consequently, they have learned how to discern between both good and evil. (Hebrews 5:13-14) The gift of discernment, on the other hand, is the supernatural ability to see beyond the physical limitations of natural vision and see what spirits are at work, whether they be angelic or demonic. They have the ability to see beyond the pretentious and identify what is truly in the heart. When Peter and John went to Samaria to follow up on the work that had been done by Philip, they encountered a convert by the name of Simon. Prior to his conversion, Simon had been a well-known sorcerer and used witchcraft to seduce the minds of the people in that city. In fact, from dignitaries to men of low degree, many people held Simon in high regard and considered him to be someone great. However, when the gospel was preached and people turned their hearts to the Lord, Simon also believed and was baptized. After he accepted Christ, Simon studied at the feet of Philip and from all appearances seemed quite sincere and devoted. Simon's true motives, for whatever reason, are not readily discerned or addressed by Philip. However, when Peter and John laid hands on the believers and they received the Holy Ghost, Simon, under the outer appearance of piety and godliness, wanted to be able to do just as the Apostles did. It is imperative that we know why a person wants to operate in a particular gift or seeks after invitations under the guise of Kingdom work. Things that look good and wholesome on the outside are not always as they appear. Much to Simon's chagrin, the gift of discernment was strong and operative in Peter, who harshly rebuked him. It was not because it is wrong to desire to lay hands on people that they might receive the Holy Ghost, but because of what was truly in Simon's heart. Peter was offended in his spirit because Simon had unwittingly thought that he had enough money to purchase the Holy Ghost who was freely given as gift to every believer. But then Peter goes beyond the surface or the physical nature of Simon and addresses his soul and spirit. "For I perceive that thou art in the gall of bitterness, and in the bond of iniquity."

(Acts 8:23) The gift of discernment penetrates the physical and examines that which is in the soul and spirit.

The gift of discerning spirits also allows the recipient to distinguish between that which is a physical problem and that which is spiritual in nature. There were times when Jesus would lay his hands on the sick and they would recover. Yet there were other times when he would address the unclean spirits or spirits of infirmity that were at work. (Mark 1:23; Mark 5:8; Luke 9:24; Luke 13:11)

THE GIFT OF FAITH

While every man has a degree of faith (Romans 12:3), not all men have the gift of faith. The measure of faith mentioned in Romans is the amount of faith necessary for salvation. Faith is substantive and produces tangible evidence regarding those things that have yet to be revealed. In the secular arena, faith is belief that is not based on proof. It is the confidence that we have in a person, place, thing, or deity. In the New Testament, faith comes from the Greek word Pistis {pis`-tis}, which means to be convinced of the truth of anything. It carries with it the idea of trust in God who cannot lie or fail to do what He has promised. In other words, faith is our reliance upon Christ for all that we need, whether physical, emotional, or spiritual. It is faith that allows the believer to trust in the immutability of Jehovah-Jireh.

The gift of faith is the supernatural ability to reach beyond the natural into the spiritual and effect changes in the physical. The spiritual gift of faith is "a sudden surge of faith, usually in a crisis, to confidently believe without a doubt, that as we act or speak in Jesus' Name it shall come to pass." (Rea, 1974) Peter and John's encounter with the lame man at the gate of the temple called Beautiful is a sterling example of the gift of faith. Without fanfare, emotionalism, or sensationalism, Peter and John step out by faith and command this paraplegic to rise up and walk. The gift of faith was not contingent upon the faith or beliefs of the lame man nor his paralytic condition. The gift of faith was not bound by three decades of atrophied limbs nor those who may have been present. The gift of faith empowers the believer to trust God for that, which is seemingly impossible. This is not a method to test God, but a means to glorify Him and in the process strengthen the body of Christ and build the faith of other believers.

THE GIFT OF HEALINGS

In the gospel according to Mark 16:18, Jesus declared that in His name believers would lay hands on the sick, and the sick would recover. While all believers have been authorized and empowered to pray for those who are sick, they do not all have the gift of healing. The spiritual gifts of healing are a supernatural phenomena that has the ability to heal physical, emotional, and spiritual maladies. Those operating in the gifts of healing will manifest this ability more often and more routinely than those who may have been used rarely or on an occasion.

There are times when people shy away from the gifts of healings in part because of the abuse that has been associated with so-called faith healers who had a propensity to take more than they gave. There are also those who are intimidated by the possibility of God not healing a person on demand. We must remember the sovereignty of God who alone makes the decision to heal or not to heal, at least not in our human estimation of healing. In our humanity, it is our desire to see people "temporarily" healed. We want them to stay in the flesh tabernacle a while longer before they die and leave our company. Although the question as to why God heals some and not others in this life is not clearly answered in the scriptures, we do know that He knows what is best in every situation. The thought processes of God are not like

The Gift of Healings

that of humanity (Isaiah 55:8). When the Lord uses a person in the gifts of healing, it should be remembered that it is His decision and His alone; and it will not only be for the benefit of the person healed, but for His honor and His glory.

THE WORKING OF MIRACLES

While there are many miraculous events throughout both the Old and New Testaments of the bible, there is not a lot of information regarding the working of miracles; many examples but no detailed explanations. The phrase working of miracles is derived from two Greek words, Energema {en-erg`-ay-mah} which means to effect operation, and Dunamis translated as explosive power. The word Dunamis is also translated to mean ability. Subsequently the working of miracles is the ability to flow and operate in the power and anointing of the Holy Ghost to effect physical, emotional, and spiritual changes that far exceed natural law.

Miracles and the working of miracles must go beyond the normal range of human ability, intellect, and resources. Miracles defy scientific reason and intellect. If the aforementioned points cannot be applied to what has been deemed miraculous, they are not miracles. The working of miracles is more than a change of disposition, attitude, or chance occurrence, but rather a phenomenon that cannot be done without divine intervention.

The working of miracles followed the ministry of the early apostles. Some of these acts went beyond the gift of healing, which in and of itself is a miracle. In the city of Lydda, there dwelt a devout woman of God who was known for her good works and acts of charity by the name of Dorcas. Despite the fact that she was a faithful disciple, Dorcas got sick and died. The saints in Lydda knew that Peter was abiding in the city, and sent for him to come without delay. When Peter came to the house where Dorcas' body was, he found her washed and prepared for burying, lying in an upper chamber. After clearing the room of everyone, Peter knelt down, prayed, and commanded Dorcas to rise and she immediately sat up. The working of miracles indeed was in operation. (Acts 9:36-41)

Paul had a similar experience when a young man by the name of Eutychus fell from the window of a third floor loft during a lengthy sermon by the apostle. Falling from such a height resulted in death. Once again, the working of miracles flowed through a believer. Rather than panicking and operating in fear, Paul embraced his lifeless body and the Holy Ghost resurrected him. (Acts 20:7-12)

The working of miracles is not for self-aggrandizement, financial gain, or adoration from others. It is always used to glorify God, to encourage the body of Christ, and point nonbelievers towards the power and love of Jesus.

CONCLUSION

The marvelous baptism in the Holy Ghost is a gift that is available to all believers and should be desired by each. It edifies, equips, and positions Christians to live victorious lives in Jesus. It increases understanding into the deeper things of God and provides pearls of wisdom, comfort, and encouragement to those who have yielded to His person. While the baptism in the Holy Spirit does not make one immune to demonic attacks, trials, tribulations, and spiritual warfare, it ensures success and positions the saints to be more than conquerors. It is this incomparable gift that endues believers with power, authority, and yoke-destroying anointing. While the believer is blessed and enjoys the favor of God, it never moves him/her to operate from a selfish or covetous position. The Holy Ghost enables a Christian to grow from the infantile milk-only consuming saint, to one who is able to digest the strong meat of the Word of God.

Dr. Frederick K. C. Price, founder and pastor emeritus of the Crenshaw Christian Center in Los Angeles, California, offers the following points on how you can be filled with the Holy Spirit:

You have to have accepted Jesus Christ as your personal savior.

CONCLUSION

Read the book of Acts and 1 Corinthians chapters 12-14, and let the word show you that the Holy Spirit is meant for every believer today.

Remember that the gift of the Holy Spirit is not given as an attainment or reward, based on some supposed degree of holiness. It is based solely on the fact that Jesus promised to give Him to every believer, freely and by grace.

When you receive the gift of the Holy Spirit, it helps to be with a group of Spirit-filled Christians who can instruct, encourage and pray with you. Although it is not essential, I personally find it to be a great help for two specific reasons. First, it is scriptural. Acts 8:17, 9:17, and 19:6 show us how others can help us by the laying on of hands as a point of faith release. Second, satan will immediately challenge you as to the authenticity of your experience, so it is good to have the witness of Christians who can affirm what has happened to you.

Now that you are ready to receive, simply pray this prayer of invitation:

"Father, I believe with all my heart, based on the scriptures, that the gift of the Holy Spirit is meant for me. Just as I have trusted you for my eternal salvation by faith, so now do I trust you, by faith to give me the fullness of the Holy Spirit with the evidence of speaking with other tongues. I now receive, by faith, the gift of the Holy Spirit. Thank you in Jesus' name."

By faith, open your mouth and yield your tongue to the Holy Spirit. Praise the Lord in tongues as the Spirit gives you the utterance. Remember, the Holy Spirit does not do the speaking – you do.

Continue to exercise your gift daily. Like an athlete preparing for competition, you must "stay in shape" by giving your new experience a daily workout. Keep praying and singing in the Spirit. If at all possible, seek other spirit-filled Christians with which to associate. And above all, find yourself a Spirit-filled church that is teaching the uncompromising, full counsel of God. That is the way to grow and stay ahead of the devil.

BIBLIOGRAPHY

Basham, Don, (1971) Tongues, interpretation, and prophecy Springdale, PA: Whitaker House.

Easton, Matthew, (1897) Bible dictionary third edition Nashville, TN: Thomas Nelson and Sons.

Finney, Charles, (1878) Finney's systematic theology Minneapolis, MN 55438: Bethany Press International.

Francis, Rodney W., (2014) The word of knowledge. Retrieved from http://www.gospel.org.nz/index.php/articles/articles-by-rodney/233-the-word-of-knowledge.

Guzik, David, The Holy Spirit is poured out on the Church. Retrieved from http://biblehub.com/commentaries/guzik/commentaries/4402.html.

Merriam-Webster (2014) Dictionary. Retrieved from http://www.merriam-webster.com/dictionary/discernment.

Price, Frederick K.C., (1996) The Holy Spirit the helper we all need Los Angeles, CA: Faith One Publishing.

Rea, John, ThD (1974) The layman's commentary on the Holy Spirit Plainfield, NJ: Logos Internaional.

Robeck, Cecil M. Jr., (2010) Montanism and present day prophets, Pneuma: The Journal of the Society for Pentecostal Studies 32:413.

Scott Foresman Dictionary.

Trinity Magazine volume 3 number 1.

Sherrill, John, (1985) They speak with other tongues.

Grand Rapids, MI: Chose Books a division of Baker Book House Company.

Vines New Testament Greek dictionary (2014) Retrieved from http://gospelhall.org/bible/bible.php?search=dorea&dict=vine&lang=greek#2.

William Seymour and the history of the Azusa street outpouring (2014) Retrieved from http://www.revival-library.org/pensketches/am_pentecostals/seymourazusa.html.

Wilson, H. Daniel, (2000) Bible study on Holy Ghost baptism Presented at Kingdom Valley Full Gospel Church, South Holland, IL.

APPENDIX

The Cloaking Device
- Mystery
- Neutralizing the Effects
- Breeds Ignorance and Confusion

A God of Order
- God, who is intricate and detailed, would never put the members of His body in a conundrum regarding His will, His word, His gifts, or His Spirit!

> *"For God is not the author of confusion, but of peace,*
> *as in all churches of the saints."*
> (1 Corinthians 14:33)

- Unfortunately, the enemy has somehow been able to distort and confuse the children of God with a gift that should bring strength and unity. Primarily because of rebellion and self-will, confusion exists.
- When we are driven by misunderstanding, a lack of Biblical knowledge, and a failure to take God at His word, we operate in a state of spiritual delusion and fall prey to heresy.

> *"Let all things be done decently and in order."*
> (1 Corinthians 14:40)

Appendix

- Needless to say, there is much confusion and disorder in the body of Christ, which has led to denominationalism and general disbelief in the household of faith!

The Promise

- The deliberate nature of God would indicate that He does everything for a purpose including the provision of the baptism in His Spirit.

> "...I will pray the Father, and He shall give you another comforter, that He may abide with you forever; even the Spirit of Truth; whom the world cannot receive, because it seeth Him not, neither knoweth Him: but ye know Him; for He dwelleth with you, and shall be in you. I will not leave you comfortless: I will come to you."
> (John 14:15-18)

- Remember, when the Lord releases a promise, our responsibility is to simply wait for the manifestation of the same.
- Unfortunately, many saints have a difficult time in the area of patience and waiting. In other words, we don't like to *"Tarry"*

> "...I send the promise of My Father upon you: but tarry ye in the city of Jerusalem, until ye be endued with power from on high."
> (Luke 24:49)

- The word "Tarry" translated from the Greek "Kathizo" (kath-id-zo), means to "sit down"!

What Is The Holy Ghost?

- The Holy Ghost is not a what – He is a Who!
- As defined by *Easton's Bible Dictionary* – "The Third Person of the Adorable Trinity. His personality is proved:

1) From the fact that the attributes of personality, intelligence and volition are acribed to Him

"...The Comforter, which is the Holy Ghost...shall teach you, and bring things to your remembrance, whatsoever I have said unto you."
(John 14:26)

"But when the Comforter is come, whom I will send unto you from the Father, even the Spirit of Truth, which proceedeth from the Father, He shall testify of me."
(John 15:26)

"But God hath revealed them unto us by His Spirit: for the Spirit searcheth all things, yea, the deep things of God. For what man knoweth the things of a man, save the Spirit of man which is in Him: even so the things of God knoweth no man, but the Spirit of God."
(1 Corinthians 2:10-11)

2) The Holy Ghost executes the offices peculiar only to a person. The very nature of these offices involves personal distinction,

"For the Holy Ghost shall teach you in the same hour what ye ought to say."
(Luke 12:12)

"And we are witnesses of these things; and so is also the Holy Ghost, whom God hath given to them that obey."
(Acts 5:32)

3) The Holy Ghost reproves, helps, glorifies, and intercedes (John 16:7-13; Romans 8:26)

Appendix

"...Nevertheless I tell you the truth: it is expedient for you that I go away: for if I go not away, the Comforter will not come unto you...when He is come He will reprove the world of sin...because they believe not on me...He will guide you into all truth...He will shew you things to come."
(John 16:7-9, 13)

"...The Spirit also helpeth our infirmities: for we know not what we should pray for...but the Spirit maketh intercession for us..."
(Romans 8:26)

- The Holy Ghost is divine (Exodus 17:7, Psalms 95:7)

"...All sins shall be forgiven unto the sons of men... but He that shall blaspheme against the Holy Ghost hath never forgiveness, but is in danger of eternal damnation."
(Mark 3:28-29)

"For there are three that bear record in Heaven, the Father, the Word, and the Holy Ghost and these three are one."
(1 John 5:7)

- He is omniscient, omnipresent, and omnipotent (1 Corinthians 2:10-11, Luke 1:35, Romans 8:11, Hebrews 2:4)

"...The Holy Ghost shall come upon thee, and the power of the highest shall overshadow thee..."
(Luke 1:35)

> *"God also bearing them witness, both with signs and wonders, and with divers miracles, and gifts of the Holy Ghost, according to His own will."*
>
> (Hebrews 2:4)

- His existence is established in the first book of the Bible. (Genesis 1:2)

> *"...The Spirit of God moved upon the face of the waters."*

The Third Figure in the Triune God
- He is God!!!
- Ruha — Hebrew for Spirit — has two meanings: 1) Wind & 2) Breath

The Holy Ghost is a Gift
(John 14:16-17, Acts 8:20)
- How do we earn or merit this gift? What do I have to do to prepare myself? How long will I have to tarry?
- Is the Holy Ghost for today, and is He for every Christian?

If the Holy Ghost is for today's saints, are there some who have not received?
- First we have to distinguish between conversion and Spirit baptism.
- Conversion (Convertere; Epistrophe)
- Baptism (Baptizein; Baptizo)

Conversion Vs. Baptism
- According to the *Scott Foresman Advanced Dictionary*, **Conversion** is defined as follows: 1) a converting; a changing or turning, change; 2) a change from unbelief to faith; changing from one religion to another. It is taken from a Latin word: ***Convertere.***
- Baptism, on the other hand, is defined as: Rite or sacrament in which a person is dipped in water or sprinkled with water, as a sign of washing away sin and admission

Appendix

into the Christian church. It is taken from the Greek word ***Baptizein***, which means to dip. The Greek lexicon defines this word as ***Baptizo***.
- (Greek): 1) to dip repeatedly, to immerse, to submerge; 2) to cleanse by dipping or submerging, to wash, to make clean with water, to wash one's self, to bathe; 3) **overwhelm**. The Greek word for conversion is ***Epistrophe***, which means conversion of Gentiles to the one true God.

The Promise of the Spirit
(John 14:16-17)
- Made by Jesus

> "And I will pray the Father, and He shall give you another Comforter, that He may abide with you forever; even the Spirit of Truth; whom the world cannot receive, because it seeth Him not, neither knoweth Him: but ye know Him; for He dwelleth with you, and shall be in you."

- Can only be received by Christians
- Indwells the believer

The Spirit is Active, Creative, and Imparts
- Genesis records that the Spirit moved upon the face of the waters.
- The Spirit created something from nothing.
- The Spirit made deposits in the creation story.
- The Spirit causes dynamic changes in everything He touches.
- The gift of the Spirit was freely given.

No More Tarrying!!!
(Acts 2:1-4)
- The promise was fulfilled when the Day of Pentecost was fully come.
- Every believer in the room was instantaneously baptized.

- They were forever changed.
- The Spirit imparted special gifts into the believer.
- Power moved from without to within the believer.

The Gifts of the Spirit
(1 Corinthians 12)

- There are nine gifts bestowed by the Spirit.
- The gifts can be divided into three categories:
    1) Gifts of inspiration/spoken
    2) Gifts of revelation
    3) Gifts of power

The Inspirational Gifts
(1 Corinthians 12:10)

> "...to another prophecy; ...to another divers kinds of tongues; to another the interpretation of tongues."

- Controversial, misunderstood, debated
- Division-confusion-disorder
- Empowerment
- Edification

Why the Controversy?

- The legalist & the doubter (1 Corinthians 14:27-28a)

> "If any man speak in an unknown tongue, let it be by two, or at the most three, and that by course; and let one interpret. But if there be no interpreter, let him keep silence in the church..."

Appendix

- The overzealous tongue talker
- Paul was a tongue talking, prophesying, miracle working apostle (1 Corinthians 13:1; 14:18)

"Though I speak with the tongues of men and of angels… I thank my God, I speak with tongues more than ye all."

- Paul supports and encourages speaking in tongues (1 Corinthians 14:5; 39b-40)

"I would that ye all spake with tongues…forbid not to speak with tongues. Let all things be done decently and in order."

Private and Public Tongues
- Private tongues – edifies the individual believer
- Public tongues – edifies the entire congregation when accompanied with the companion gift of interpretation
- The believer is yet in control (1 Corinthians 14:32)

The Gift of Tounges
- A sign that the Spirit has entered the believer (not necessarily the only sign)
- Assists the believer in praising God and leads him to pray for that which he does not understand
- Provides direct communication between God and man

Heavenly Language
- Tongues have often been described as direct communication with God and the believer through the Holy Spirit

"For he that speaketh in an unknown tongue speaketh not unto men, but unto God; for no man understandeth Him: Howbeit in the Spirit he speaketh mysteries."
(1 Corinthians 14:2)

"If you praise Him in the private language of tongues, God understands you but no one else does, for you are sharing intimacies just between you and Him."
(1 Corinthians 14:2, Message version)

- There are times when believers are so pressed or excited in the spirit until they don't truly know what to pray for

"Likewise the Spirit also helpeth our infirmities: for we know not what we should pray for as we ought: but the Spirit itself maketh intercession for us with groaning which cannot be uttered."
(Romans 8:26)

"Meanwhile, the moment we get tired in the waiting, God's spirit is right alongside helping us along. If we don't know what to pray, it doesn't matter. He does our praying in and for us, making prayer out of our wordless sighs, our aching groans."
(Message version)

- According to Ken Woolridge, Ministries International, there are four kinds of tongues manifest in the Assembly:
  1) Exhortation
     The Spirit speaks to the Church words of comfort, edification and encouragement. This requires the accompanying gift of interpretation.
  2) Rebuke
     The Spirit reveals, rebukes and attacks satanic forces against the church or believers.

3) Intercession

The Spirit intercedes on behalf of a person, a situation or the whole meeting of believers where prayer is urgently required. Interpretation is not always required.

4) Praise

The Spirit introduces, directs, effects or harmonizes praise within the assembly of believers. (Again, interpretation is not always necessary.)

Speaking in Tongues (Personal V. Private)

- Personal tongues are private and used in devotion/prayer life

"I thank my God, I speak with tongues more than ye all."
(1 Corinthians 14:18)

- Tongues may be spoken in private and God sometimes gives the individual interpretation for his own edification.

"For if I pray in an unknown tongue, my Spirit prayeth,
but my understanding is unfruitful. What is it then? I will pray with the Spirit,
and I will pray with the understanding also…"
(1 Corinthians 14:14-15)

- Personal or private tongues are actually Spirit to spirit communications. God's Spirit is in you talking and communicating with your spirit, and receiving the praise.

"He that speaketh in an unknown tongue speaketh not unto men, but unto God:
for no man understandeth Him; howbeit in the Spirit he speaketh mysteries.

"Praying always with all prayer and supplication in the spirit…"
(Ephesians 6:18)

- Tongues may be spoken in private and God gives the individual interpretation for His own edification.
- Just because you speak in tongues in the privacy of personal devotion doesn't mean that God will always give you the interpretation, which should not be viewed as a problem.
- Remember, Romans 8:26 reminds us that, *"...the Spirit itself maketh intercession for us with groanings which cannot be uttered."*

Public Tongues

- Because a tongue is publicly heard doesn't make it public. It becomes public when it is spoken for the benefit of those in attendance.
- When a public tongue is presented, it should be accompanied by interpretation.

> *"I would that ye all spake with tongues, but rather that ye prophesied: for greaters is he that prophesieth than he that speaketh with tongues, except he interpret, that the church may receive edifying."*
> (1 Corinthians 14:5)

- Personal tongues as a form of prayer may be spoken as long as it's done decently and in order.
- Tongues may be spoken in public without an interpreter as long as it is not glaring, disruptive, or out of order. There are times during public worship in which tongues may go forth during corporate prayer or praise/worship.

> *"Even so ye, forasmuch as ye are zealous of spiritual gifts, seek that ye may excel to the edifying of the church. Wherefore let him that speaketh in an unknown tongue pray that he may interpret...brethren, be not children in understanding...in understanding be men...tongues are for a sign, not to them that believe, but to them that believe not..."*
> (1 Corinthians 14:12, 13, 20, 22)

- When tongues go forth publicly and it's glaring, exceeding the normal current word level of the service, one should begin to pray for the interpretation; for there should be a message in this tongue for the whole church; or the individual should be silent.

Interpretation of Tongues
- While not every word spoken in an unknown tongue is to be interpreted, there are times when the Spirit of God will provide an understanding to what has been spoken for the edification of the entire assembly.

> *"If any man speak in an unknown tongue, let it be by two, or at the most by three, and that by course; and let one interpret. But if there be no interpreter, let him keep silence in the church; and let him speak to himself, and to God."*
> (1 Corinthians 14:27-28)

- We must remember that the Apostle Paul never forbade speaking in tongues. He did, however, provide instructions for the orderly presentation of tongues and interpretation.
- We must remember that order and decency should not be abandoned because of spiritual immaturity.
- The recipient of tongues and interpretation are in control of the free exercise of God's gifts.
- The gifts of God never get out of order with the will of God, we must, therefore, always be in order!

The Gift of Prophecy

> *"Follow after charity, and desire spiritual gifts, but rather that ye may prophesy…but he that prophesieth speaketh unto men to edification, and exhortation, and comfort."*
> (1 Corinthians 14:1 & 3)

- Three primary functions:
    1. Edification
    2. Exhortation
    3. Comfort
- Prophecy is not psychic friends!

Edification
- Moral improvement; spiritual benefit; instruction; to *uplift*
- In 1 Corinthians 14:3, the word edification is derived from the Greek *Oikodome (oy-kod-om-ay)*, which means *the act of one who promotes another's growth in Christian wisdom.*

Exhortation
- Strong urging; earnest advice or warning!
- Exhortation is translated from the Greek Paraklesis (par-ak-lay-sis) and refers to a persuasive discourse or stirring address. It is instructive, admonitory (mild rebuke), and conciliatory.

Comfort
- Ease the grief or sorrow
- Anything that makes trouble or sorrow easier to bear
- Consolation
- From the Greek word Paramuthia (par-am-oo-thee-'ah), comfort literally is to calm!
- According to Ken Woolridge, Ministries International, prophecy has two additional purposes:
    1) It ordains and sends
    2) It ministers to unbelievers
- In 1 Timothy 4:14, Paul says, *"Neglect not the gift that is in thee, which was given thee by prophecy, with the laying on of the hands of the presbytery."*

Appendix

*"Do not neglect your gift, which was given you through
a prophetic message when the body of elders laid their hands on you."*
(1 Timothy 4:14 NIV)

- "When unbelievers are present in the church, the Holy Spirit may minister to them through prophecy." (Woolridge, 2002))

*"But if all prophesy, and there come in one that believeth not,
or one unlearned, he is convinced of all, he is judged of all: and thus are the secrets
of his heart made manifest; and so falling down on his face he will worship God,
and report that God is in you of a truth."*
(1 Corinthians 14:24-25)

- Great care and caution must be exercised in protecting the gift of prophecy from those who would pervert, manipulate, and abuse it and the people to whom it is directed.
- When people stand and declare, "Thus saith the Lord," we should be attentive and scrutinize every word!

"Let the prophets speak two or three, and let the other judge."
(1 Corinthians 14:29)

Prophecy is Not God Gossiping!
- Prophecy is not manipulative
- It is not self-serving
- It is never destructive
- The prophet cannot be a "loose cannon"

"And the spirits of the prophets are subject to the prophets."
"The spirits of the prophets are subject to the control of prophets."
(1 Corinthians 14:32 NIV)

Gifts of Revelation

> *"For to one is given by the Spirit the word of wisdom; to another the word of knowledge by the same spirit;...to another discerning of the spirits."*
> (1 Corinthians 12: 8 & 10b)

- The Revelation gifts include:
    - Word of Wisdom
    - Word of Knowledge
    - The Discerning of Spirits

Word of Wisdom

> *"So that thou incline thine ear unto wisdom, and apply thine heart to understanding...for the Lord giveth wisdom: out of his mouth cometh knowledge and understanding."*
> (Proverbs 2:2 & 6)

- Wisdom is the proper application of knowledge.
- In other words, the Holy Spirit tells us what to do with knowledge.
- It is divine application of information!

> *"A word of wisdom is a tiny fragment and portion of God's immeasurable wisdom given at a specific time, for a specific situation. By using this gift, the Holy Spirit supernaturally affects people, situations and things and brings about His desires and purposes."*
> (Woolridge)

- It is the Spirit of God that reveals to us what our course of action should be.

Appendix

"Trust in the Lord with all thine heart; and lean not unto thine own understanding. In all thy ways acknowledge Him, and He shall direct thy paths."
(Proverbs 3:5-6)

Word of Knowledge

- While the gift of knowledge is akin to a word of wisdom, they differ in that knowledge exposes something that has already happened or revealed whether known or unknown to the hearer. It is informational.
- Nathan's revelation to David regarding Bathsheba was a word of knowledge.
- A word of knowledge is not prophetic!
- There are five reasons why the Holy Spirit uses a word of knowledge to and through us (Woodridge):
    1) To warn people
    2) To inform people
    3) To expose hidden things
    4) To confirm things
    5) To reveal God's power in knowing secrets

"And thus are the secrets of his heart made manifest; and so falling down on his face he will worship God, and report that God is in you of a truth."
(1 Corinthians 14:25)

Discerning of Spirits

"To another the working of miracles; to another prophecy; to another discerning of spirits..."
(1 Corinthians 12:10)

- The word discerning is translated from the Greek word Diakrisis (dee-ak-ree-sis), which means the ability to distinguish between divers spirits.

- We must remember that the devil is a master of disguise.

> *"For satan himself is transformed into an angel of light."*
> (2 Corinthians 11:14)

- Because the adversary has but a short time, he has become far more sophisticated and camouflaged in his presentation to the saints of God. Consequently, the ability to discern spirits is crucial to survival.
- We have become mesmerized by the world and its riches and have not concerned ourselves with the spirit which we are dealing.

> *"Beloved, believe not every spirit, but try the spirits whether they are of God: because many false prophets are gone out into the world."*
> (1 John 4:1)

- The gift of discernment enables the believer to detect the presence of demons as well as angels or ministering spirits.
- It also identifies those who are being used by the Lord or by demonic forces.
- This gift allows the recipient to see people as they truly are. It may also reveal demonic activity or unclean spirits that may be at work, in addition to hurts, wounds, fears, depression, and torment.
- It is not a judgmental spirit and therefore the believer must be careful to operate in the spirit and not in their own imaginations or emotions!
- Peter used the spirit of discernment to see the true character of Simon the Sorcerer.

> *"Thy heart is not right in the sight of God. Repent therefore of this thy wickedness, and pray God, if perhaps the thought of thine heart may be forgiven thee, for I perceive that thou art in the gall of bitterness, and in the bond of iniquity."*
> (Acts 8:21b-23)

APPENDIX

- Discernment also reveals positive attributes such as faith.

> *"The same heard Paul speak: who steadfastly beholding him, and perceiving that he had faith to be healed."*
> (Acts 14:9)

The Gifts of Power

> *"To another faith by the same spirit; to another the gifts of healing by the same spirit; to another the working of miracles…"*
> (1 Corinthians 12:9-10)

- The power gifts include:
    1) Faith
    2) Healing
    3) Miracles

The Gift of Faith

- In the book of Romans 12:3, the word of God declares,

> *"For I say, through the grace given unto me, to every man that is among you, not to think of himself more highly than he ought to think; but to think soberly, according as God hath dealt to every man the measure of faith."*
> (Romans 12:3)

- There is a difference between the *measure of faith* and the *gift of faith*.
- In addition to the measure of faith, Romans 10:17 refers to yet another type of faith.

> *"So then faith cometh by hearing, and hearing by the word of God."*
> (Romans 10:17)

- Even though all three forms of faith are translated from the same Greek word Pistis, their meanings and purpose are vastly different.
  - Measure of Faith – is faith to be saved.
  - General Faith – grows and is a result of hearing the word.
  - Gift of Faith – supernatural
- The gift of faith supernaturally empowers the believer to do that which defies logic, natural laws, and the extraordinary.
- The gift of faith works hand in hand with gifts of miracles and healings.
- Casting out demons, raising the dead, and working miracles are manifestations of the gift of faith.
- The creation story is a prime example of the gift of faith.

"Through faith we understand that the worlds were framed by the word of God, so that things which are seen were not made of things which do appear."
(Hebrews 11:3)

The Gift of Healing

"...To another the gifts of healing by the same spirit."
(1 Corinthians 12:9)

- Throughout the Bible, God has always shown Himself to be a healer.

"...If thou will diligently hearken to the voice of the Lord thy God, and wilt do that which is right in His sight, and will give ear to His commandments, and keep all His statutes, I will put none of these diseases upon thee, which I have brought upon the Egyptians: for I am the Lord that healeth thee."
(Exodus 15:26)

- In Exodus, God declares Himself to be Jehovah–Rapha!

APPENDIX

- The gift of healings should not be mysterious to the born again believer, when you consider that Jesus' ministry was characterized by spiritual and physical healings.
- While every believer has been empowered by the Holy Ghost to lay hands on the sick, the gift of healing is not given to every Christian.
- The Apostles continued healing the sick throughout their ministries.
- The gift of healing is often used in conjunction with a word of knowledge and discernment.
- Some illnesses are caused by diseases, germs and defects in organs, while others are the result of a spirit of infirmity or other demonic activities.
- Regardless as to the source of the malady, the Holy Ghost has empowered certain saints to operate in the gift of healing, which is not contingent upon the services of Earthly physicians.
- Sadly, many 21st century Christians don't believe healing occurs today!
- The gift of healing can be hindered by doubt and unbelief.

> *"And he could there do no mighty work, save that he laid his hands upon a few sick folk, and healed them. And he marveled because of their unbelief…"*
> (Mark 6:5-6a)

- When Jesus healed/resurrected the daughter of Jairus, He put the doubters and naysayers out.
- When the Lord uses a believer in the gift of healing, it is the Lord and not the believer who gets the glory!

The Gift of Miracles

> *"To another the working of miracles…"*
> (1 Corinthians 12:10a)

- Interestingly enough, the word miracles is derived from the same Greek word for power, *Dunamis*, which also means *strength* and *ability*!
- The working of miracles is a supernatural energy from God that causes an instantaneous creative change in the human body, nature or a specific situation. It is described as a mighty work. (Woolridge)

"…When He was come into His own country,
He taught them in their synagogue, insomuch that they were astonished, and said,
whence hath this man this wisdom, and these mighty works?"
(Matthew 13:54)

- The gift of miracles was often used by God to validate the ministries of His chosen.
- Moses calls down plagues upon Egypt.
- Elijah shuts up the heavens for a space of three years.
- Jesus turns water into wine, walks on water, and feeds the multitude with two fish and five loaves of bread.
- When the sleeping saint, Eutychus, fell from the third loft and was killed, Paul miraculously puts the life back in him with an embrace. (Acts 20:9-10)
- The ministry of the Apostles were characterized by miracles.

"And by the hands of the apostles were many signs and wonders wrought among
the people; (and they were all with one accord in Solomon's porch.)"
(Acts 5:12)

"Then Simon himself believed also; and when he was baptized, he continued with
Philip, and wondered, beholding the miracles and signs which were done."
(Acts 8:13)

- Remember, signs and wonders are supposed to follow us, we don't follow the signs and wonders!!!

APPENDIX

Harmony of the Nine Gifts

• According to Woolridge, there are four essential methods by which the gifts of the spirit operate:

1) By the anointing of the Holy Spirit

"How God anointed Jesus of Nazareth with the Holy Ghost and with power: who went about doing good, and healing all that were oppressed of the devil; for God was with Him."
(Acts 10:38)

2) By being sensitive to the Holy Spirit

"He that hath an ear, let him hear what the Spirit saith unto the churches."
(Revelation 3:6)

"For as many as are led by the Spirit of God, they are the sons of God."
(Romans 8:14)

3) By faith

"He therefore that ministereth to you the Spirit, and worketh miracles among you, doeth he it by the works of the law, or by the hearing of faith?"
(Galatians 3:5)

4) By love – everything we do for God is packaged in love.

"But speaking the truth in love, may grow up into him in all things, which is the head, even Christ."
(Ephesians 4:15)

- To be baptized in the Holy Ghost and not have, demonstrate and operate in love is a contradiction of terms.
- Believers who are truly spirit filled are characterized by their capacity to love!

> *"Those who do not operate in love, are irritating noisy workers and are counted as nothing."*
> (Woolridge)

> *"Though I speak with the tongues of men and of angels, and have not love, I am become as sounding brass or tinkling cymbal. And though I have the gift of prophecy, and understand all mysteries, and all knowledge; and though I have all faith, so that I could remove mountains, and have not love, I am nothing."*
> (1 Corinthians 13:1-2)

Movement of the Spirit Leaves a Deposit

> *"And the earth was without form, and void; and darkness was upon the face of the deep. And the Spirit of God moved upon the face of the waters."*
> (Genesis 1:2)

- When the believer is baptized (Baptizo) in the Spirit, deposits of spiritual gifts are left inside (nine different gifts).
- Adam was a lump of clay until the movement of the Spirit from external to internal. (Genesis 2:7)

Where's the Proof?

- Evidence is anything that shows what is true and what is not; facts; proof!!!
- The baptism in the Holy Ghost must be validated by the conspicuous operative functioning of spiritual gifts.

APPENDIX

- Am I baptized in the Holy Ghost if I don't speak in tongues? Throughout scriptures there is a common trait amongst those who have been in the direct presence of God. Their lives were irrefutably changed!
- Since the Holy Ghost is God, and to be baptized by Him is to be overwhelmed by Him, a change must occur.
- There is no baptism without some type of evidence.
- When Jesus was baptized by John in the Jordan River, God audibly and with a visual sign validated his ministry.

> *"...When He was baptized, went up straightway out of the water: And, lo, the heavens were opened to Him, and He saw the Spirit of God descending like a dove, and lighting upon Him: and lo, a voice from heaven, saying, this is My beloved Son, in whom I am well pleased."*
> (Matthew 3:16-17)

- Whereas our opinions may be important to us and a few others, evidence erases doubt, fear and erroneous teachings!
- Evidence shows what is true and what is not; it provides facts and confidence.
- A lack of evidence leads to doctrines and beliefs for which there is no scriptural support.
- Scriptures do not support the notion that tongue talking is the only form of evidence. Remember, there are nine gifts of the Spirit, nine different deposits!
- In recorded cases of Holy Ghost baptism in the New Testament, the recipients usually spoke in tongues.
- While some conjecture that scriptures are quiet concerning the initial baptism of the Holy Ghost experienced by the Apostle Paul, the record is clear that he did speak in tongues.

> *"I thank my God, I speak with tongues more than ye all."*
> (1 Corinthians 13:18)

- Because the gifts of the Spirit are supernatural endowments, it would stand to reason that the evidence must also be supernatural.
- Don't confuse salvation with Holy Ghost baptism!
- The scriptures do not support the notion that tongue talking is evidence of salvation.
- We are encouraged by the Word of God to not be ignorant of spiritual gifts, but to desire and use the better gifts.

"But covet earnestly the best gifts: and yet shew I unto you a more excellent way."
(1 Corinthians 12:31)

Gifts Have A Purpose!
- In ministering the gifts of the Holy Spirit, we always need to focus on two things:
    1) Edifying the church

*"Even so ye, forasmuch as ye are zealous for spiritual gifts,
seek that ye may excel to the edifying of the church."*
(1 Corinthians 14:12) (Woolridge)

    2) Defeating satan and his kingdom

*"And these signs shall follow them that believe;
in my name shall they cast out devils; they shall speak with new tongues;
they shall take up serpents; and if they drink any deadly thing, it shall not hurt
them; they shall lay hands on the sick, and they shall recover."*
(Mark 16:17-18) (Woolridge)

- The gifts of the Spirit should be used in harmony for the honor and glory of God.
- God does not endow us with spiritual gifts to glorify ourselves!

Appendix

It's Not About You!

- Our desire for and use of spiritual gifts should be to show the light of Jesus and His sacrifice for His glory and honor!!!

> *"As every man hath received the gift, even so minister the same one to another, as good stewards of the manifold grace of God. If any man speak, let him speak as the oracles of God; if any man minister, let him do it as of the ability which God giveth: that God in all things may be glorified through Jesus Christ, to whom be praise and dominion for ever and ever. Amen."*
>
> (1 Peter 4:10-11)

- The gifts of the Spirit must be viewed in the context of love as opposed to an exclusionary badge used to separate believers along denominational and doctrinal lines!

> *"That there should be no schism in the body; but that the members should have the same care one for another."*
>
> (1 Corinthians 12:25)

- Whereas the baptism of the Holy Ghost unifies, strengthens, and edifies believers, it is an outward expression to the world of our covenant relationship with Christ!
- Operating in spiritual gifts allows the power of God to transform ministries from impotent social clubs into ministries that are powerful enough to turn the world upside down!

> *"…These that have turned the world upside down…"*
>
> (Acts 17:6b)

- It is the deposit of spiritual gifts activated by the anointing that empowers the saints to become soul winners and to impact the physical realm by spiritual means.

> *"For the weapons of our warfare are not carnal, but mighty through God to the pulling down of strong holds."*
>
> (2 Corinthians 10:4)

Love, the Common Thread!
- Because the entire Word of God and His relationship to man is based on love, it only stands to reason that spiritual gifts without love are ineffective and detrimental to the testimony of the saints.

> *"Though I speak with the tongues of men and of angels, and have not charity, I am become as sounding brass, or a tinkling cymbal. And though I have the gift of prophecy, and understand all mysteries, and all knowledge; and though I have faith, so that I could remove mountains, and have not charity, I am nothing."*
>
> (1 Corinthians 13:1-2)

- Remember, we are not saved because we are baptized in the Holy Ghost, we are baptized in the Spirit because we are saved.
- In other words, salvation is a prerequisite to being baptized in the Holy Ghost.
- Conversion and the baptism of the Spirit are separate and distinct experiences, although they can occur within the same time frame.
- The experience of being spirit filled is reserved for those who not only believe in the Lord, but who have accepted Him as Lord and Savior!
- While those who have been endowed with spiritual gifts are certainly blessed to be filled with the Holy Ghost, our focus must not be on the gift, but the Giver and His purpose for our lives.
- The fact that God baptized us with the Holy Ghost is not evidence of our salvation, but of His ever-abiding presence in our spirits.

A Change In Status
- Salvation changes our status, station, and position with God and destiny.

Appendix

- We are miraculously transformed from sinner to saint.
- The baptism of the Holy Ghost is the actual occupation of the saints by the Lord Himself (this process does not prevent us from being free moral agents; but rather empowers us to walk in the power and authority set aside for the sons of God).

*"…As many as received Him, to them gave He power
to become the sons of God…"*
(1 John 1:12)

"For as many as are led by the Spirit of God, they are the sons of God."
(Romans 8:14)

Salvation

- Salvation comes through no other name than Jesus.

*"Neither is there salvation in any other…there is none other name under heaven
given among men, whereby we must be saved."*
(Acts 4:12)

- Salvation comes with a commandment to go!!!

"…Go ye into all the world…"
(Mark 16:15)

- Jesus is the truth.

"Jesus saith…I am the way, the truth, and the life…"
(John 14:6)

- The gospel is the power of salvation.

> *"I am not ashamed of the gospel of Christ...*
> *it is the power of God unto salvation..."*
> (Romans 1:16)

The Baptism of the Spirit

- On the day of Pentecost, 120 saved believers were filled (baptized) with the Holy Ghost.

> *"And they were all filled with the Holy Ghost,*
> *and began to speak with other tongues..."*
> (Acts 2:4)

- The Samaritans saved under the preaching of Philip were not filled until Peter and John laid hands on them.

> *"(For as yet He was fallen upon none of them: only they were*
> *baptized in the name of the Lord Jesus.) Then laid they their hands on them,*
> *and they received the Holy Ghost."*
> (Acts 8:16-17)

- Paul was not baptized with the Holy Ghost until Ananias laid hands on him.

> *"...Ananias went his way, and entered into the house;*
> *and putting his hands on him said, Brother Saul, the Lord, even Jesus,*
> *that appeared unto thee in the way as thou camest, hath sent me, that thou*
> *mightest receive thy sight, and be filled with the Holy Ghost."*
> (Acts 9:17)

- Cornelius, years after the day of Pentecost, was converted and later baptized in the Spirit (and spoke with tongues).

APPENDIX

"While Peter yet spake these words, the Holy Ghost fell on all them which heard the word…on the Gentiles also was poured out the gift of the Holy Ghost. For they heard them speak with tongues…"
(Acts 10:44-46)

- The Ephesian disciples were baptized unto John's baptism, but did not receive the baptism of the Holy Ghost until they were baptized in Jesus name and after Paul laid hands on them.

"…Paul having passed through the upper coasts came to Ephesus: and finding certain disciples, he said unto them, have ye received the Holy Ghost since ye believed? And they said…We have not so much as heard whether there be any Holy Ghost…they were baptized in the name of the Lord Jesus…and when Paul had laid his hands upon them, the Holy Ghost came on them; and they spake with tongues and prophesied."
(Acts 19:1, 2, 5, 6)

Ten Reasons Why Saints Should Desire To Speak In Tongues

1) One of the most obvious signs that a saint was spirit filled was speaking in tongues as the Spirit gave utterance.

"…They were all filled with the Holy Ghost, and began to speak with other tongues, as the Spirit gave them utterance."
(Acts 2:4)

"For they heard them speak with tongues, and magnify God…"
(Acts 10:46)

2) God, through the Apostle Paul, encouraged the Corinthian church to speak in tongues.

"I would that ye all spake with tongues…"
(1 Corinthians 14:5)

*"But ye, beloved, building up yourselves on your most holy faith,
praying in the Holy Ghost."*
(Jude 20)

3) Speaking in tongues keeps us continually aware of the Holy Spirit's indwelling presence.

4) Speaking in tongues eliminates the possibility of selfishness entering our prayer life.

*"Likewise the Spirit also helpeth our infirmities:
for we know not what we should pray for as we ought: but the Spirit itself maketh intercession for us with groanings which cannot be uttered."*
(Romans 8:26)

5) Believers should desire to speak in tongues because it helps them learn to trust God even more.

*"But ye, beloved, building up yourselves on your most holy faith,
praying in the Holy Ghost."*
(Jude 20)

*"Trust in the Lord with all thine heart;
and lean not unto thine own understanding."*
(Proverbs 3:5)

6) Speaking in tongues is a means of keeping us free from contamination from the ungodly and profane elements of the world (I/You can pray in tongues alone).

Appendix

"But if there be no interpreter, let him keep silence in the church;
and let him speak to himself, and to God."
(1 Corinthians 14:28)

7) The believer should desire to speak in tongues because it provides a way for things to be prayed for which no one thinks to pray about.

8) A very good reason to speak in tongues is the refreshing and rest that comes with it.

"...With men of other tongues and other lips will I speak unto this people..."
(1 Corinthians 14:21)

"...With stammering lips and another tongue will
He speak to this people, to whom He said, this is the rest wherewith ye may cause
the weary to rest: and this is the refreshing..."
(Isaiah 28:11-12)

9) As believers, we have been commanded to give thanks for all things. Speaking in tongues is a way to give thanks.

"What is it then? I will pray with the Spirit,
and I will pray with the understanding also: I will sing with the Spirit,
and I will sing with the understanding also. Else when thou shalt bless with the
Spirit, how shall he that occupieth the room of the unlearned say amen, at thy
giving of thanks, seeing he understandeth not what thou sayest? For thou verily
givest thanks well, but the other is not edified."
(I Corinthians 14:15-17)

10) The final reason every believer should desire to speak in tongues is found in James 3:8. **"But the tongue can no man tame; it is an unruly evil full of deadly poison."**

- Yielding your tongue to the Holy Spirit to speak with other tongues is a big step toward being able to fully yield all of your members to God, for if you can yield your tongue, you can yield any member of your body.

Prayer of Invitation

"Father, I believe with all my heart, based on the scriptures, that the gift of the Holy Spirit is meant for me. Just as I have trusted you for my eternal salvation by faith, so now do I trust you, by faith, to give me the fullness of the Holy Spirit with the evidence of speaking with other tongues. I now receive, by faith, the gift of the Holy Spirit."
(Dr. Fredrick K.C. Price)

SCRIPTURAL REFERENCES

1 Corinthians
2:10-11 .... 25, 27, 117, 118
2:11 .... 25, 27
2:13 25
6:19 39
11 25
11:13-15 74
12 .... 53, 77, 85, 121
12:8 .... 93, 94, 96
12:8-9 78
12: 8 & 10b 129
12:9 133
12:9-10 132
12:9-11 27
12:10 .... 85, 121, 130
12:10a 134
12:11 25
12:13 27
12:25 .... 25, 140
12:31 139
13 60
13:1 122
13:1-2 .... 137, 141
13:8 57
13:18 138
14:1 & 3 126
14:2 .... 56, 63, 80, 82, 123
14:3 & 4 .... 72, 80, 127
14:5 .... 70, 80, 122, 125, 145
14:12 .... 80, 125, 139
14:13 .... 80, 125
14:13-15 56
14:14 82
14:14-15 .... 80, 124
14:15-17 83
14:18 .... 69, 122, 124
14:20 .... 80, 125
14:21 .... 82, 146
14:21-22 .... 55, 56, 80
14:22 125
14:24-25 128
14:25 130
14:27-28 .... 59, 88, 126
14:27-28a 121
14:28 .... 57, 146
14:29 128
14:29-31 72
14:29-32 91

Scriptural References

14:32 .... 64, 122, 128
14:33 .... 18, 115
14:37-40 80
14:39 63
14:39b-40 122
14:40 .... 63, 90, 115

1 John
1:7-9 39
1:12 142
4:1 131
5:7 .... 29, 118
5:14-15 66

1 Peter
4:10-11 140

1 Thessalonians
5:19 57
5:23 30

1 Timothy
4:14 .... 127, 128

2 Corinthians
10:4 141
11:14 131

2 Peter
1:21 25

2 Samuel
12 95

Acts
1:8 21
2 .... 52, 55, 56
2:1-4 .... 52, 120
2:4 .... 53, 81, 82, 85, 143, 144
2:14-40 56
2:17-18 33
2:38, 39, & 38-39 ...34, 35, 36, 40
4:12 .... 81, 142
5:1-11 95
5:12 135
5:32 .... 25, 117
6:3 94
8 69
8:5-17 81
8:13 135
8:16-17 143
8:17 110
8:20 .... 29, 41, 119
8:21b-23 131
8:23 101
8:27-40 97
9:3-18 81
9:17 .... 110, 143
9:17-18 85
9:36-41 108
10 37

10:28 91
10:34 48
10:38 136
10:44-46 .... 81, 144
10:44-47 .... 38, 85
10:46 .... 82, 144
11:14 81
14:9 132
14-21 85
15:28-29 26
17:6b 140
19:1, 2, 5, 6 144
19:1-6 85
19:1-7 .... 44, 81, 90
19:2 21
19:6 110
20:7-12 108
20:9-10 135
28:25 27

Ephesians
2:8 39
2:8-9 40
2:17 27
2:18 27
4:11-12 87
4:15 136
4:24 &29 80
6:18 .... 80, 124

Exodus
15:26 133
17:7 .... 26, 118

Galatians
3:5 136

Genesis
1:2 .... 27, 71, 119, 137
2:7 137
3:4-5 74
40 93
41 .... 93, 94

Hebrews
2:4 .... 25, 26, 27, 118, 119
3:7 25
3:7-11 26
5:13-14 99
6:13-18 35
11:3 133
11:6 41

Hosea
4:6 44

Scriptural References

Isaiah 96
   6:3 27
   28:11-12 .... 80, 82, 146
   46:10 90
   55:8 106
   55:11 48

James
   3:8 .... 83, 147

Job
   26:13 27
   33:4 28

John
   1:45-50 96
   4:23 83
   14:6 .... 81, 142
   14:15-18 116
   14:16 51
   14:16-17 .... 29, 51, 119, 120
   14:17, 26 25
   14:26 117
   15:26 .... 25, 117
   16:7-9, 13 118
   16:7-13 .... 25, 117

Jude
   20 .... 80, 82, 145

Luke
   1:35 .... 27, 118
   9:24 101
   12:12 .... 25, 117
   13:11 101
   14:49 52
   24:49 116

Mark
   1:23 101
   3:24-26 54
   3:28-29 118
   5:8 101
   6:5-6a 134
   9:23 .... 48, 53
   16:15 142
   16:15-16 81
   16:17 75
   16:17-18 .... 80, 139
   16:18 105

Matthew
   3:16-17 138
   12:28 27
   13:54 135
   16:4 74
   28:19 .... 27, 91

Numbers
   23:19 37

Proverbs

2:2 & 6 129
3:5 .... 82, 145
3:5-6 130

Psalms

95:7 .... 26, 118
104:30 27
107:2 79
139:7 27

Revelation

1:4 27
3:6 136

Romans

1:16 143
8:11 .... 27, 118
8:14 .... 136, 142
8:26 .... 25, 64, 80, 82, 84, 117,
            118, 123, 125, 145
9:1 27
10:17 132
12:1 83
12:3 .... 103, 132

BIBLICAL FIGURES AND PLACES

A
Abraham 34, 35
Adam 74, 137
Ananias 69, 81, 95, 143
Apollos 44
Arius 23

B
Bathsheba 95, 130

C
Caesarea 65
Christ 9, 10, 13, 15, 17, 21, 23, 25, 38, 39, 44, 53, 54, 72, 74, 77, 81, 85, 87, 88, 94, 97, 99, 100, 103, 104, 108, 116, 136, 140, 143
Corinth 44, 59
Cornelius 37, 38, 81, 91, 143

D
Damascus 60
David 79, 95, 130
Devil 111, 131, 136, 139
Dorcas 108

E
Egypt 94, 135
Elijah 135
Ephesus 44, 45, 144
Eutychus 108, 135
Eve 74

G
Garden of Eden 74
God 17, 18, 22, 23, 24, 25, 26, 27, 29, 30, 31, 32, 33, 34, 35, 36, 37, 38, 39, 40, 41, 43, 44, 45, 48, 49, 51, 52, 53, 54, 55, 56, 57, 60, 63, 64, 65, 66, 67, 69, 71, 72, 73, 74, 77, 78, 79, 82, 83, 85, 86, 87, 88, 89, 90, 91, 92, 93, 95, 96, 103, 104, 105, 107, 108, 109, 111, 115, 117, 119, 120, 122, 123, 124, 125, 126, 128, 129, 130, 131, 132, 133, 135, 136, 137, 138, 139, 140, 141, 143, 144, 145, 146, 147

Biblical Figures and Places

H

Holy Ghost 13, 14, 15, 16, 17, 18, 21, 22, 23, 24, 25, 26, 27, 28, 29, 31, 32, 33, 34, 35, 36, 37, 38, 39, 40, 41, 43, 44, 45, 47, 49, 52, 53, 57, 63, 64, 65, 67, 69, 70, 77, 78, 82, 89, 90, 93, 94, 95, 100, 107, 108, 109, 116, 117, 118, 119, 134, 136, 137, 138, 139, 140, 141, 143, 144, 145

Holy Spirit 14, 21, 23, 27, 29, 32, 34, 41, 43, 44, 45, 47, 49, 51, 55, 57, 60, 65, 66, 70, 72, 77, 81, 82, 83, 85, 88, 90, 91, 92, 93, 96, 97, 109, 110, 122, 128, 129, 130, 136, 139, 145, 147

Holy Trinity 27

I

Isaiah 96

Israel 94

J

Jairus 134

Jehovah 27, 65, 133

Jehovah-Jireh 66, 103

Jeremiah 79

Jerusalem 52, 65, 69, 96, 116

Jesus 21, 22, 23, 25, 29, 30, 34, 37, 39, 40, 44, 48, 51, 52, 53, 54, 63, 74, 92, 94, 95, 96, 101, 103, 105, 108, 109, 110, 134, 135, 136, 138, 140, 142, 143, 144

John 29, 44, 51, 69, 81, 99, 100, 103, 138, 143, 144

Jonas 74

Jordan River 138

Joseph 93, 94

L

Lydda 107, 108

M

Montanus 22

Moses 79, 95, 135

N

Nathan 95, 130

Nathanael 95, 96

Nazareth 95, 136

Numbers 23:19 37

P

Paul 26, 44, 45, 53, 59, 60, 63, 64, 65, 69, 70, 71, 72, 74, 78, 82, 85, 90, 93, 108, 122, 126, 127, 132, 135, 138, 143, 144

Peter 26, 29, 34, 37, 38, 40, 41, 48, 56, 65, 69, 91, 95, 99, 100, 103, 108, 131, 143, 144

Pharaoh 79, 94

Philip 81, 96, 97, 100, 135

S

Samaria 69, 100

Samuel 79

Sapphira 95

Saul 143

Simon the Sorcerer 29, 41, 69, 131

T

Triune God 21, 24, 27, 28, 77

V

Virgin Mary 25

INDEX

A

Admonishment 66
Anointing 12, 13, 37, 45, 65, 107, 109, 136, 140

B

Baptism 15, 16, 21, 32, 33, 35, 37, 39, 40, 43, 44, 45, 47, 48, 49, 53, 60, 69, 77, 79, 109, 116, 119, 137, 138, 139, 140, 141, 142, 144
Barnett, Betty Jo 9
Barnett, Betty Mae Ridley 10
Barnett, Burdis Jr. 10
Barnett, Carol Jean Grundy 10
Basham, Don 71
Bathsheba 95, 130

C

Carbondale, Illinois 11
Chicago, Illinois 10, 79
Christian Valley Full Gospel Church 79
Clemons, Marva Watson 9
Conversion 43, 49, 60, 119

Corinth 44, 59
Crenshaw Christian Center 109

E

Edification 72, 73, 121, 123, 127
Exhortation 66, 72, 73, 123, 127

F

Finney, Charles 36
Francis, Rodney W. 96

G

Gilley, Gary 21, 22
Glossolalia 21, 33, 47, 78, 79
Godhead 22, 23
Graham, Billy 12
Grundy, Mattie 9
Guzik, David 55

K

Kingdom of God 13

L

Los Angeles, California 109

Index

P
Pneuma 28, 29, 30, 31, 33, 34, 39, 63, 66

Price, Dr. Fredrick K.C. 85, 109, 147

R
Ruah 28, 39, 48, 51

S
Sabellius 22

Seymour, William 47

Sherrill, John 28, 64, 65, 70

Simon, Yolanda 10

Socinus, Fausto 24

Soroti, Uganda 88

Southern Illinois University 11, 13

Speaking in Tongues 21, 33, 47, 55, 60, 66, 70, 78, 79, 82, 83, 89, 124, 144, 145, 146

Spirit of God 12, 13, 15, 16, 28, 64, 65

St. John Praise & Worship Center Ministries International 9

T
Tamms, Illinois 13, 14

Trinity 23, 25, 116

V
Van Impe, Jack 12

W
Watson, Calvin 9

Wilson, H. Daniel 79

Woolridge, Ken 123, 127

ABOUT THE AUTHOR

In addition to serving in ministry for nearly forty years, Dr. Larry T. Barnett, Sr. has been the Senior Pastor of *St. John Praise & Worship Center Ministries* (SJPWC) for more than thirty years. Although SJPWC is located in rural Southern Illinois, it has a global vision and outreach, international as well as national. He is a sought-after preacher, teacher, and speaker both in the United States and abroad. Pastor Barnett, as he prefers to be called, teaches leadership seminars and conducts open air crusades in Kenya, Tanzania, and Uganda with many signs, wonders, and miracles validating the anointing that God has placed upon his life. In conjunction with the Honorable Bishop Dr. Joseph Macharia Wambugu, founder of *Bread of New Life Ministries*, Pastor Barnett has been blessed to make a notable impact in East Africa.

Amongst his other duties and responsibilities, Dr. Barnett is the assistant presiding Bishop of Covenant Ministries under the direction of the Honorable Bishop Dr. Ron Webb. He teaches a variety of subjects at the *School of the Prophets Bible College* in Poplar Bluff, Missouri, and has been blessed to share the gospel in many states.

About the Author

Dr. Barnett has served as a building administrator in public schools in Illinois for nearly thirty years. During his tenure as an educator he also had the distinction of serving as an athletic director and head basketball coach. His love for the game of basketball afforded him the opportunity to be a basketball referee at the high school and collegiate level for thirty-five years. He holds a Bachelor and Master of Science in Education. He earned a Bachelor and Master of Science and Theological Doctorate in Christian Education and Leadership. He is married to the beautiful and lovely Carol J. Barnett and they have been blessed with five wonderful children, Cala (who has gone home to be with the Lord), Shaya (husband Michael), T.J. (wife Christina), Sean (wife Christine), and Donte. They also have two wonderful grandchildren, Daja and Michael, Jr. They have truly been blessed by the BEST!

For speaking engagements and ministry information Dr. Barnett can be reached at:

(618) 342-6785
larry.barnett@excite.com or SJPWC.ORG
PO Box 226
Pulaski, IL 62976

Note from the Publisher

Are you a first time author?

Not sure how to proceed to get your book published?
Want to keep all your rights and all your royalties?
Want it to look as good as a Top 10 publisher?
Need help with editing, layout, cover design?
Want it out there selling in 90 days or less?

Visit our website for some exciting new options!

www.chalfant-eckert-publishing.com

www.ingramcontent.com/pod-product-compliance
Lightning Source LLC
Chambersburg PA
CBHW052036070526
44584CB00016B/2068